THE ART OF WOODWORKING

ADVANCED ROUTING

THE ART OF WOODWORKING

ADVANCED ROUTING

TIME-LIFE BOOKS
ALEXANDRIA, VIRGINIA

ST. REMY PRESS
MONTREAL

THE ART OF WOODWORKING was produced by
ST. REMY PRESS

PUBLISHER	Kenneth Winchester
PRESIDENT	Pierre Léveillé
Series Editor	Pierre Home-Douglas
Series Art Director	Francine Lemieux
Senior Editor	Marc Cassini
Editor	Andrew Jones
Art Directors	Jean-Pierre Bourgeois, Michel Giguère
Designers	François Daxhelet, Hélène Dion, Jean-Guy Doiron
Picture Editor	Christopher Jackson
Writers	John Dowling, Adam Van Sertima
Contributing Illustrators	Gilles Beauchemin, Michel Blais, Ronald Durepos, Michael Stockdale, James Thérien
Administrator	Natalie Watanabe
Production Manager	Michelle Turbide
Coordinator	Dominique Gagné
System Coordinator	Eric Beaulieu
Photographer	Robert Chartier
Indexers	Ann Hamilton, Christine M. Jacobs

Time-Life Books is a division of Time Life Inc.,
a wholly owned subsidiary of
THE TIME INC. BOOK COMPANY

TIME-LIFE INC.

President and CEO	John M. Fahey
Editor-in-Chief	John L. Papanek

TIME-LIFE BOOKS

President	John D. Hall
Vice-President, Director of Marketing	Nancy K. Jones
Managing Editor	Roberta Conlan
Director of Design	Michael Hentges
Director of Editorial Operations	Ellen Robling
Consulting Editor	John R. Sullivan
Vice-President, Book Production	Marjann Caldwell
Production Manager	Marlene Zack
Quality Assurance Manager	James King

THE CONSULTANTS

Ted Fuller is the product manager at Delta International Machinery/Porter Cable (Canada). He is currently working in new product development and marketing for woodworking tools and equipment.

Giles Miller-Mead taught advanced cabinetmaking at Montreal technical schools for more than ten years. A native of New Zealand, he has worked as a restorer of antique furniture.

Patrick Spielman is an authority on routing and shaping and is the author of over 30 books on woodworking, including *The New Router Handbook*, published by Sterling Press. He operates a shop and lives in Fish Creek, Wisconsin.

The Art of woodworking. Advanced routing.
p. cm.
Includes index.
ISBN 0-8094-9541-4
1. Routers (Tools)
2. Woodwork.
I. Time-Life Books.
II. Series: Art of woodworking.
TT203.5.A78 1995
684'.083—dc20   95-12164
                                    CIP

For information about any Time-Life book,
please call 1-800-621-7026, or write:
Reader Information
Time-Life Customer Service
P.O. Box C-32068
Richmond, Virginia
23261-2068

CONTENTS

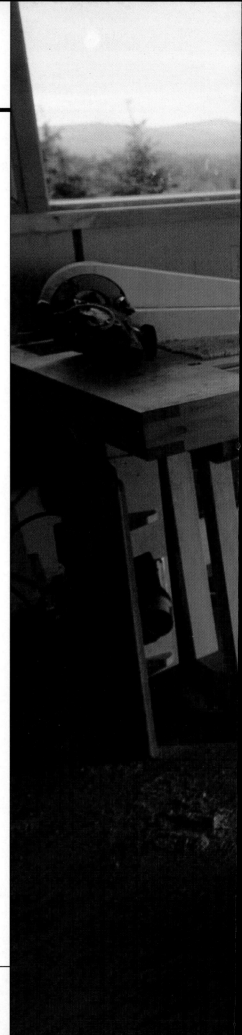

Howard Wing on
THE EVOLUTION OF ROUTING

When I started working with wood half a century ago, the electric router saw only limited use in small shops. The machines were short on power and adjustments often proved difficult to make. And the bits! The high-speed steel bits dulled so quickly that you learned to sharpen them or made a cloud of fine sawdust instead of curly shavings. One advantage of steel was that you could grind your own cutter shapes; but you had to do that anyway because there just weren't that many profiles available. And instead of a pilot bearing there was a steel post on the end of the bit that rode on the work, leaving a nice burnished surface just below the cut that had to be sanded out. When I used a router then it was generally to round over or chamfer an edge because it gave such a nice crisp result.

Five decades later, my old $^7/_8$-horsepower, silver-colored router is still around and makes an occasional cut in my shop, but it's been joined by a trio of big, versatile machines that do the real work. Technology has changed the routing and shaping scene with a vengeance. Bearing failures, once common, are rare with soft-start electronics. Meanwhile, multiple speeds let me use large-diameter bits, and plunge routers have eliminated the hazards of "tipping in" to the work.

Then come the cutters which, after all, are the reason the machines exist. With few exceptions they all have carbide cutting edges that last forever, and there are literally hundreds of shapes available, many with pilot bearings that let me faithfully follow a master pattern. On the shelf over my working routers are racks with enough standard and specialized profiles to let me take on any job.

Today, the focus has moved from the machines and bits to devising clever ways of holding the work and the router. A cottage industry of ingenious clamps, jigs, and "ultimate" router tables has sprung up, and I can now make one or many parts with repeatable accuracy better than the smallest divisions on my ruler. But, as good as the router world seems, I can still wish for better things. Most important, I'd like routers to be quieter and cleaner. The noise stems partly from the machine and partly from the bit, so both need work, but wouldn't it be nice to run a router without ear protection?

And don't forget those cutters. There are always more profiles to be made but I think the real changes lie in reduced tearout and improved cut quality. We're already seeing ideas like spiral edges that shear cut and limited-feed shapes that really work, so there may be a whole world of new improvements out there—so many that I expect to look back in another 10 years and say, "that's the way things were before routers got really good."

Howard Wing left an engineering career to be a self-taught furniture maker specializing in "fairly complicated geometric and organic shapes with a contemporary flair." He lives in Hartland, Vermont.

Martin Godfrey invents
THE WOODRAT

Received wisdom has it that necessity is the mother of invention, but my best ideas seem to come from an idle mind, and are usually relevant to subjects I know little about. The WoodRat, mounted on the shop wall behind me in the photo at left, came from just such an idle thought: Although I was well taught at school, I had not cut a dovetail since then, and I wanted to find a better way of routing them.

Yet working with the router is to a large extent a business of making jigs, and jig-making often takes over from the work at hand and becomes an end in itself. I envisioned a single jig to hold both the wood *and* the router, replacing the need for multiple jigs. I called it the WoodRat.

Having an idea that no one else in the whole wide world has had is a euphoric experience. The whole wide world, on the other hand, is often managing quite well without it. Why are they not beating a pathway to my door to buy me out? I feel a bit like a mad inventor.

My original prototype, made seven years ago from scrap plastic and wire, works well enough. The excitement of making that first rough box has driven the business ever since. Then the discovery process begins, and I became a Development Engineer, learning too much to be mad anymore. By holding stock vertically in the jig, I found that I could rout practically any length of timber. Introducing a Bowden cable allowed stock to be power fed smoothly *with* the direction of bit rotation, reducing tearout and prolonging bit life. And once the dovetails are all sorted out, I discovered that the Rat has no difficulty making any other joint in the book. Suddenly one can make fine furniture without a seven-year apprenticeship.

Gathering forward momentum, I switched hats with each new stage: production manager, photographer, copywriter, businessman (complete with suit), and technical writer. I am not qualified for any of this but no one else does a better job for no pay. Was this what I intended when it all began?

But there are milestones, like the first fellow that pays with a wad of notes, the smell of brochures fresh from the printers, trying out new parts hot from the mold (Do they fit? Yes!), the thousandth sale. It's a heady moment when the U.S. patent arrives, and I join the ranks of patient scientists, dreamers, and cranks. It is the only kind of diploma there is, since there is no school for inventors. A little respect here, please.

There must come a point where the WoodRat gets taken on worldwide by an outfit with more marketing clout than I have. Bowing out will be a wrench, but then everyone is having fun with my machine except me. I shall happily go back to my workshop, where there are some projects that I've just been having some idle thoughts about.

Martin Godfrey is a woodworker and inventor
who lives near Wells in Somerset, England.

Clive Joslin on
TIMBER FRAMING WITH THE ROUTER

My first encounter with timber framing was 13 years ago, when a friend enlisted me on raising day to help him erect the frame that he had spent the better part of the summer carving. It was a 2,500-square-foot saltbox with a one-story shed on one of the gable ends. At the end of the day I stood in awe at the magnificent structure before us. Timber frames are their most spectacular at this point. Standing alone, the visual appearance of the frame exudes strength and durability.

As we closed in the house over the next few months, I had numerous occasions to admire the joinery and contemplate simpler methods of mortising. Where the tenon work demands no more than a circular saw and the occasional hand saw when the depth of cut exceeds the power tool's limit, mortising the traditional way requires hours of mallet and chisel work. I knew that with routers I could accomplish the task quicker and probably more accurately.

Timbers for a frame are normally rough sawn, so mortises can vary considerably for similarly dimensioned timber, creating the need for a jig design with a high degree of flexibility. With a very simple jig made from $^1/_4$-inch-thick aluminum angle, I can quickly set up to rout an infinite variety of mortise sizes. The basic requirement is to extend the bearing surface beyond the edge of the timber to allow guide fences to be clamped, and to provide support for the router base.

I do the bulk of my mortising with $^1/_2$-inch straight bits, leaving a $^1/_4$-inch radius on the corners. Rather than square all these corners with a chisel I've found it easier to grind the radius on the tenons and corners of the beams to be housed. On deeper mortises—up to $3^1/_2$ inches—two different-length bits must be used. The degree of accuracy and precision achieved with the routers allows cleaner mortises that are truly perpendicular to the surface. This pays off when fitting knee braces and tightening the frame prior to pegging. The accuracy of the knee braces in particular is critical to the alignment and structural integrity of the frame.

Being able to mortise simply and quickly, even through large knots, makes it easy to fully house all tenons, increasing the overall strength of the frame and giving a cleaner look to the joinery. In a typical frame there can be 200 to 300 mortises. With routers I can cut my mortising time in half or better. That adds up to a substantial saving in the production of a frame, and the joints' greater precision makes a much more pleasant raising day.

Clive Joslin is a professional carpenter who lives in Hudson, Quebec.

ROUTERS AND ACCESSORIES

Jigs are essential for making a router both a safer and a more versatile tool. The workpiece handler shown above on the right is ideal for feeding small stock across a router table while keeping the operator's hands clear of the bit. The shop-made fence on the left provides a bearing surface for the workpiece and partially guards the bit.

The router is arguably the most versatile and efficient power tool in the modern woodshop. A standard fixed-base router with a straight bit can plow rabbets, grooves, and dadoes in seconds. Fitted with an edge-forming bit, the tool can round over a tabletop or shape a piece of elaborate molding. Coupled with a jig, the router turns into a joint-making dynamo, capable of producing dovetails, box joints, or mortise-and-tenons with more speed and precision than virtually any other single tool in the shop.

Many of these tasks once required hours of laborious hand work. Although some traditionalists bemoan the fact that the router has motorized the pleasure out of many woodworking tasks, others see it as a tool of liberation. The router's system of bits, cutters, and accessories has freed the modern woodworker from the arduous monotony of many repetitive procedures.

This chapter is an introduction to the two major types of routers on the market and a survey of some helpful com-

mercial jigs that expand the tools' capabilities. Whether you choose a fixed-base router or a plunge model—or both—selecting the best tool to suit your particular needs is of paramount importance. The relative strengths and weaknesses of the two types are discussed on page 14.

Whichever tool you decide to select, make sure the motor is capable of at least 1 horsepower. Also, spend the few extra dollars for a tool with adjustable speed—large-diameter cutters work best at slow speeds, while smaller-diameter bits operate better at high speeds.

While routers do not generally require much maintenance, the steps for keeping them working safely and accurately are easy to perform. The chapter explains, for example, how to check the collet for runout *(page 18)*. The chapter concludes with a few general principles on making basic edge-forming and grooving cuts—the foundations of the advanced operations that are covered in detail in later chapters.

Fitted with a piloted three-wing slotting cutter, a router plows a groove in the edge of a board. The cutter's pilot bearing rides along the stock to ensure that the cutting depth remains uniform.

ANATOMY OF A ROUTER

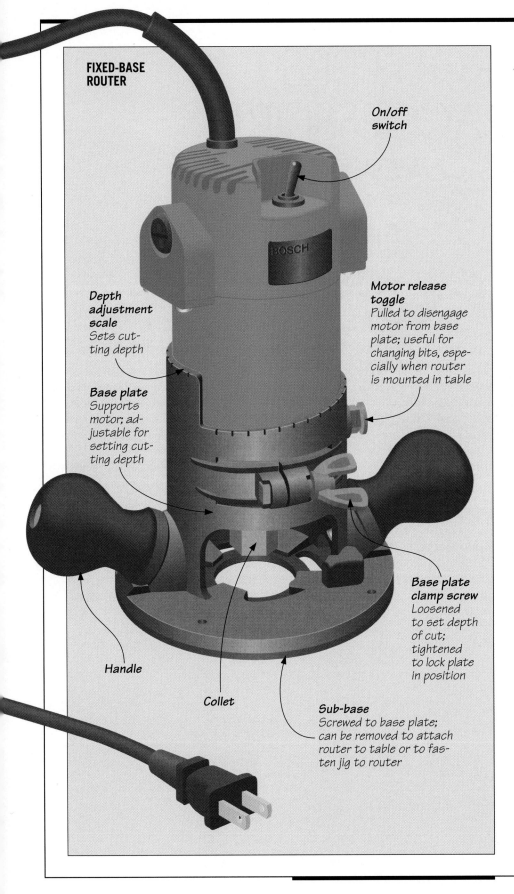

FIXED-BASE ROUTER

On/off switch

Depth adjustment scale
Sets cutting depth

Base plate
Supports motor; adjustable for setting cutting depth

Motor release toggle
Pulled to disengage motor from base plate; useful for changing bits, especially when router is mounted in table

Base plate clamp screw
Loosened to set depth of cut; tightened to lock plate in position

Handle

Collet

Sub-base
Screwed to base plate; can be removed to attach router to table or to fasten jig to router

Although the fixed-base router has been available for most of this century, the plunge router is a more recent invention, dating back only 30 years. But its popularity has grown exponentially in the past decade.

Each type of router has its strengths. For hand-held routing, a fixed-base tool, like the one shown at left, is a good choice. Fixed-base models are lighter, adjust more simply, and are generally less expensive than plunge routers of comparable size and power. Because of their simplicity, fixed-base routers work well with a router table; in most cases, separating the motor barrel from the base plate can be accomplished by loosening a screw and twisting.

For plowing grooves and mortises, on the other hand, a plunge router, like the model illustrated opposite is a good option. This type of router allows you to plunge the bit into the stock to a predetermined depth with the sub-base flat on the surface. With a fixed-base router, the tool must be held with the bit clear of the stock, turned on, and then pivoted into the surface.

Either type of router performs well in edge-forming operations. When selecting a router, consider the following options and features: The tool should have variable speed; bits should be easy to change; the sub-base should be perfectly flat; the on/off switch should be easy to operate with both hands on the tool; and the router should be substantial and durable.

If you are choosing a plunge model, check for a smooth plunge action and a plunge lock that is comfortable to engage while operating the tool. Well-designed models should allow you to make minute adjustments to the plunge depth with little fuss.

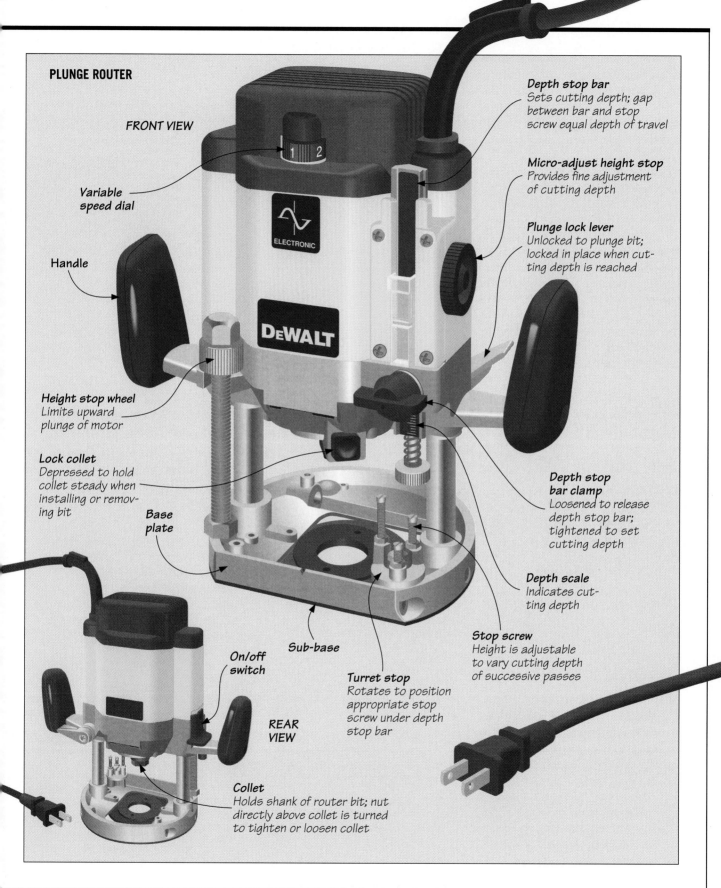

PLUNGE ROUTER

FRONT VIEW

Depth stop bar
Sets cutting depth; gap between bar and stop screw equal depth of travel

Micro-adjust height stop
Provides fine adjustment of cutting depth

Plunge lock lever
Unlocked to plunge bit; locked in place when cutting depth is reached

Variable speed dial

ELECTRONIC

Handle

DeWALT

Height stop wheel
Limits upward plunge of motor

Lock collet
Depressed to hold collet steady when installing or removing bit

Base plate

Depth stop bar clamp
Loosened to release depth stop bar; tightened to set cutting depth

Depth scale
Indicates cutting depth

Sub-base

On/off switch

REAR VIEW

Turret stop
Rotates to position appropriate stop screw under depth stop bar

Stop screw
Height is adjustable to vary cutting depth of successive passes

Collet
Holds shank of router bit; nut directly above collet is turned to tighten or loosen collet

ROUTER ACCESSORIES

As the router's popularity has grown, so have the number of commercial jigs designed to enhance its capabilities. Some of these products are shown at right. Simple and inexpensive devices, such as the corner-rounding or circle jig, enable routers to accomplish tasks that would be impossible to perform free-hand. Some of these accessories, like the foot switch, make the tool more convenient to use. Others, such as the vacuum attachment, make the router a cleaner and safer tool.

Some accessories refine the router's cutting capabilities. Template guides, for example, allow you to duplicate the profile of a pattern. A few of the devices on the market, like the molding jig, are designed to transform the router into another tool altogether.

A SAMPLING OF ROUTER ACCESSORIES

Molding jig
For cutting moldings;
router is fastened upright
in jig, which is moved along workpiece

Template guides
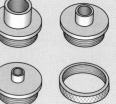
Used for pattern routing, the guides ride along a template, enabling the bit to replicate the pattern; sized for different-diameter bits, threaded part is secured to router base plate by locking ring (bottom, right)

Universal sub-base
Used to attach router to table or accessories to base plate; slots make sub-base compatible with any router model

Spacer fence
Attached to router table to facilitate the cutting of finger or box joints. The bit extends through hole; ridge serves as a key, maintaining uniform distance between notches

Substituting for a standard sub-base, the offset base shown above features a handle that helps keep the router flat on the workpiece while the bit shapes an edge. Made of transparent acrylic plastic, the jig makes it possible to view the operation. Its larger surface area makes the router more stable when performing edge-forming operations. The jig was designed by Pat Warner of Escondido, California.

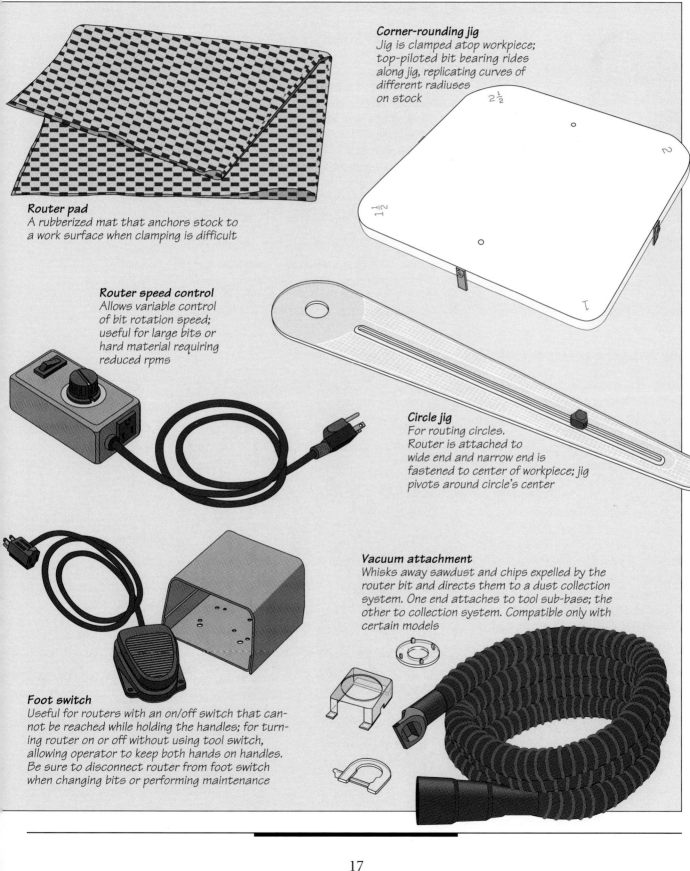

Corner-rounding jig
Jig is clamped atop workpiece;
top-piloted bit bearing rides
along jig, replicating curves of
different radiuses
on stock

$2\frac{1}{2}$

2

$1\frac{1}{2}$

1

Router pad
A rubberized mat that anchors stock to
a work surface when clamping is difficult

Router speed control
Allows variable control
of bit rotation speed;
useful for large bits or
hard material requiring
reduced rpms

Circle jig
For routing circles.
Router is attached to
wide end and narrow end is
fastened to center of workpiece; jig
pivots around circle's center

Vacuum attachment
Whisks away sawdust and chips expelled by the
router bit and directs them to a dust collection
system. One end attaches to tool sub-base; the
other to collection system. Compatible only with
certain models

Foot switch
Useful for routers with an on/off switch that cannot be reached while holding the handles; for turning router on or off without using tool switch,
allowing operator to keep both hands on handles.
Be sure to disconnect router from foot switch
when changing bits or performing maintenance

MAINTENANCE AND SAFETY

Spinning at speeds of up to 25,000 revolutions per minute, a router can cause a significant amount of damage—both to its operator and the workpiece—if it is poorly maintained. Fortunately, keeping a router in top working order is simple and takes relatively little time. Start by keeping your router bits and accessories clean, and by sharpening cutting edges as required. Periodically checking a router collet for runout, as shown below, will allow you to determine whether your bits are spinning true.

There are two main hazards associated with routing, in addition to the obvious risks posed by the spinning cutter: the noise generated by the tool, and flying chips and dust. You can counter each of these risks by wearing hearing and eye protection when operating a router and by connecting the tool to your shop dust collection system, as shown in the photo at left. Other routing safety tips are presented on page 19. Keep in mind that sharp bits will generate fewer and smaller chips than dull cutters.

Most of the wood chips and sawdust generated by the plunge router shown at left are captured by a vacuum attachment. Hooked to the tool's base plate, the flexible hose carries the chips and dust to a collection bag.

CHECKING FOR COLLET RUNOUT

Using a dial indicator and magnetic base
Install a centering pin in the router as you would a bit and set the tool upside down on a metal surface, such as a table saw. Connect a dial indicator to a magnetic base and place the base next to the router. Turn on the magnet and position the router so the centering pin contacts the plunger of the dial indicator. Calibrate the dial indicator to zero following the manufacturer's instructions. Then turn the shaft of the router by hand to rotate the centering pin *(right)*. The dial indicator will register collet runout—the amount of wobble that the collet is giving the bit. If the runout exceeds 0.005 inches, replace the collet.

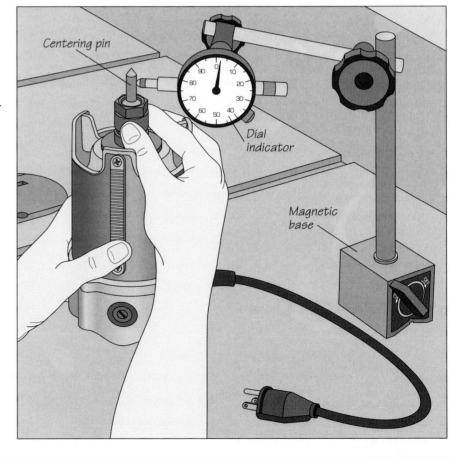

Centering pin

Dial indicator

Magnetic base

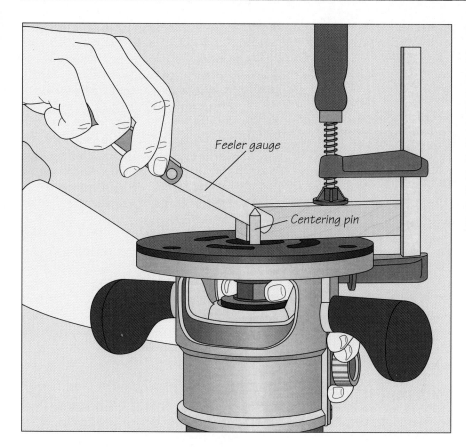

Feeler gauge

Centering pin

Using a feeler gauge

If you do not have a dial indicator, you can test for collet runout with a feeler gauge and a straight wood block. With the centering pin in the collet and the router upside down on a work surface, clamp the block lightly to the tool's sub-base so the piece of wood touches the pin. Turn the router shaft by hand; any runout will cause the pin to move the block. Then use a feeler gauge to measure any gap between the pin and the block *(left)*. If the gap exceeds 0.005 inch, replace the collet.

ROUTING SAFETY TIPS

• Wear safety glasses, a dust mask and hearing protection whenever operating a router.

• Keep bits clean and sharp; discard any that are chipped or damaged.

• Periodically check the collet for runout and keep the collet clean.

• Keep a push stick nearby to complete cuts on a router table.

• Always feed work against the rotation of the cutters.

• When routing freehand, clamp stock to a work surface.

• For deep cuts, make several passes, increasing the cutting depth gradually, rather than trying to reach your final depth in a single pass.

SHOP TIP

Checking a collet for slippage

To determine whether your router bits are slipping in the collet, install a bit and mark a line with a felt pen along the bit shank and collet. Then make a few cuts on a scrap board and examine the line. The marks on the bit and collet should remain perfectly aligned. If they have shifted apart, the bit has slipped in the collet. Remove the bit and clean any pitch or sawdust out of the collet with a fine-bristled brass brush. Re-install the bit, making sure it is well tightened, and retest. Replace the collet if the marks shift again.

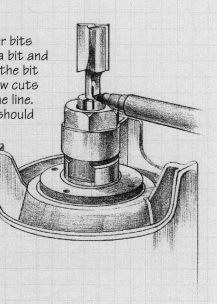

Whether you are shaping the edges of a tabletop with a decorative bit or routing a recess in the middle of a workpiece for a piece of inlay, all cuts with a router are guided by the same basic principles. For starters, the speed at which the bit rotates depends on the size of the cutter. As shown in the chart below, the larger the bit, the slower the bit rotation should be. Always adjust the speed dial on your router to suit the bit diameter before starting a routing operation.

Feed direction is another important consideration in router work. Proper technique will help you maintain control of the tool. As a rule, the router should be moved against the direction of bit rotation, or from left to right when facing the work's edge, as shown in the illustration below.

Setting the cutting depth on a fixed-base router like the one shown above involves setting the tool upside down on a work surface, placing the workpiece on the sub-base, loosening the clamp screw, and turning the depth adjustment knob until the tip of the bit aligns with the depth line.

ROUTER BIT ROTATION

BIT DIAMETER	MAXIMUM FREE-RUNNING SPEED
up to 1 inch diameter	22,000-24,000 rpm
1¼ to 2 inch diameter	18,000 rpm
2¼ to 2¼ inch diameter	16,000 rpm
2½ to 3¼ inch diameter	8,000-12,000 rpm

ROUTER FEED DIRECTION

Router feed direction

For most operations, guide the router into a workpiece against the direction of bit rotation. This will pull the bit into the wood and help prevent the router from "climbing" the workpiece and pulling away from you. On an outside edge, move the router in a counterclockwise direction; on an inside edge, feed the tool clockwise *(right)*. Start with cuts that are against the grain so you can eliminate any tearout with the cuts along the grain that follow. Position yourself to pull the router toward you, rather than pushing the tool.

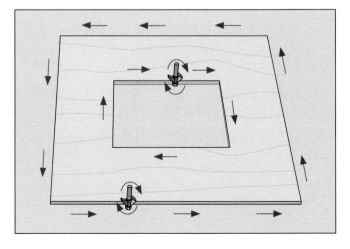

BASIC ROUTING

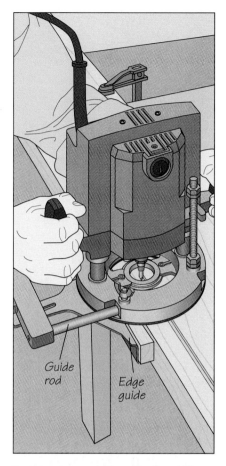

Guide rod

Edge guide

Shaping an edge with a piloted bit
Clamp down the workpiece with the edge to be shaped extending off the work surface by a few inches. Gripping the router firmly with both hands, set its sub-base on the workpiece with the bit clear of the stock. Turn on the tool and guide the bit into the workpiece until the pilot bearing contacts the stock, keeping the sub-base flat on the surface and the bearing flush against the edge *(above)*.

SHOP TIP

Setting the cutting depth on a plunge router
Make a series of wood blocks so the thickness of each one equals a cutting depth you commonly use. Then position the shortest stop screw on the turret stop directly under the depth stop bar. Seat the bar on the stop screw, then push the motor down until the bit contacts the workpiece. Next, raise the stop bar and slip the appropriate block between the bar and the stop screw *(right)*. Tighten the depth stop bar clamp and loosen the plunge lock lever, allowing the bit to spring back up. When you plunge the bit into the stock, it will penetrate until the stop bar contacts the stop screw—a distance equal to the thickness of the wood block.

Routing a groove with a non-piloted bit
Install a commercial edge guide on the router, inserting the guide rods into the predrilled holes in the tool's base plate. Align the bit with the groove outline, then butt the guide fence against the edge of the stock. Pressing the fence flush against the edge, start the cut at one end of the workpiece and feed the router along the surface *(above)*.

ROUTER BITS

Lubricating a router bit with a silicone-based lubricant before and after using it will help prevent the cutter from overheating.

A router is only as good as the bit it turns. The quality of the cuts you make will depend largely on the quality of the bits you use. Recent developments in bit-making technology have increased the likelihood that your bits will begin sharp and stay sharp. And they have expanded the choices available to woodworkers, although those extra options can sometimes seem more confusing than helpful.

The first decision involves choosing the appropriate material for the bit. Most cutters are made from either high-speed steel (HSS) or high-speed steel with carbide cutting edges. HSS bits are adequate for working with softwood, but they will not stand up well to long-term use in dense hardwood. While carbide-tipped bits are more expensive and prone to chipping, they stay sharp longer and cut more easily through harder wood.

Many experts argue that machined bits are better made than cast router bits, and double-fluted bits cut more smoothly than single-fluted cutters. Quality is, of course, important. Before buying a bit, make sure the shank is perfectly straight. A bit that does not spin true will shudder, producing a rough, imprecise cut. On carbide-tipped bits, also inspect the brazing bond between the cutting edge and the shank. A bit with an uneven bond may fly apart under the stress of a cut. Other features are worth considering. For example, a bit boasting a nonstick coating like Teflon™ will take longer to become gummed up with pitch. As shown on page 25, you can also choose between piloted and non-piloted bits, cutters that feature anti-kick-back characteristics, and bits with spiral cutters.

Bits with different shank sizes perform different jobs. To shape an edge with a hand-held router, for example, a 1/4-inch bit is usually appropriate. If you are using a bit with a 1/2-inch-diameter shank, mounting the router in a table will yield the best results. Large bits can be difficult to control in a hand-held router. Instead of using one large bit, however, you can make consecutive passes with two smaller bits.

This chapter illustrates several of the more popular bit profiles and shows the shape each type cuts in wood. Edge-forming bits are presented beginning on page 26, grooving bits are shown on page 28, and router table bits follow on page 30. Useful tips on sharpening and maintaining bits are provided starting on page 32.

The staircase handrail shown at left was shaped by making two cuts with different piloted bits mounted in a table-mounted router. A handrail bit shaped the bottom portion of the piece and a table-and-handrail cutter rounded over the top.

CHOOSING ROUTER BITS

There are several characteristics to look for when buying router bits; each of them is shown below and on page 25. As it cuts through wood, a bit should only contact the workpiece with its cutting edges; the body should never touch the wood. As shown in the photo at left, you can check for this feature by measuring the cutting circle of the bit—the distance between the cutting edges—and the wing diameter. In a properly made bit, the cutting circle diameter exceeds the body diameter; the difference is known as side clearance.

A bit should also slice through wood with the edge of the cutter rather than the face. Two features make this possi-

A set of calipers measures the side clearance of a router bit, or the difference in diameter between the bit's cutting swath and the bit body. In a bit with adequate clearance, the bit body will not contact the workpiece as the cutting edges remove the waste.

ble. The first is the hook angle, which is the angle formed by the intersection between the cutting edge and the spinning axis of the bit. The second is bit shear, as illustrated on page 25. On bits with shear, the cutting edge is tilted vertically with respect to the shank. Bits with shear and a hook angle of about 20° will produce a smooth cut with little tearout and are less likely to cause kickback.

Bits with anti-kickback, or chip-limiting, designs are becoming increasingly common. The cutters on these bits protrude from the bit body by only one-half as much as on a standard bit. By taking a shallower bite, the bits place less strain on the router motor. In addition, the bodies of these bits are virtually solid, with only a small gap between each cutting edge and the bit body. This reduces the risk of kickback.

Some straight bits are manufactured with a spiral design. Upcut spiral bits remove waste faster because they expel wood chips upward. Downcut spiral bits are slower, but they provide a cleaner cut.

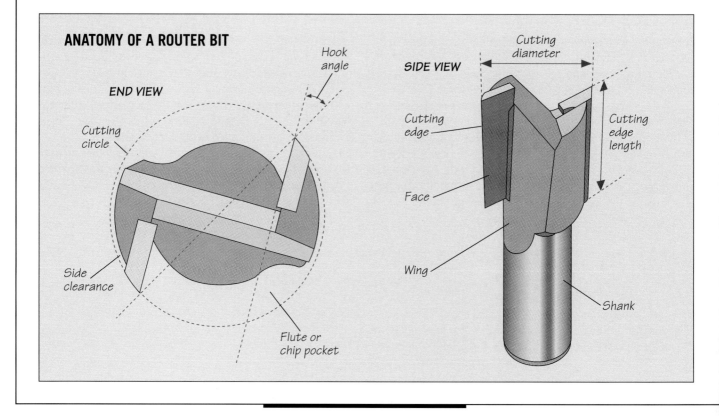

ANATOMY OF A ROUTER BIT

END VIEW

Hook angle

Cutting circle

Side clearance

Flute or chip pocket

SIDE VIEW

Cutting diameter

Cutting edge

Face

Wing

Cutting edge length

Shank

BIT CHARACTERISTICS

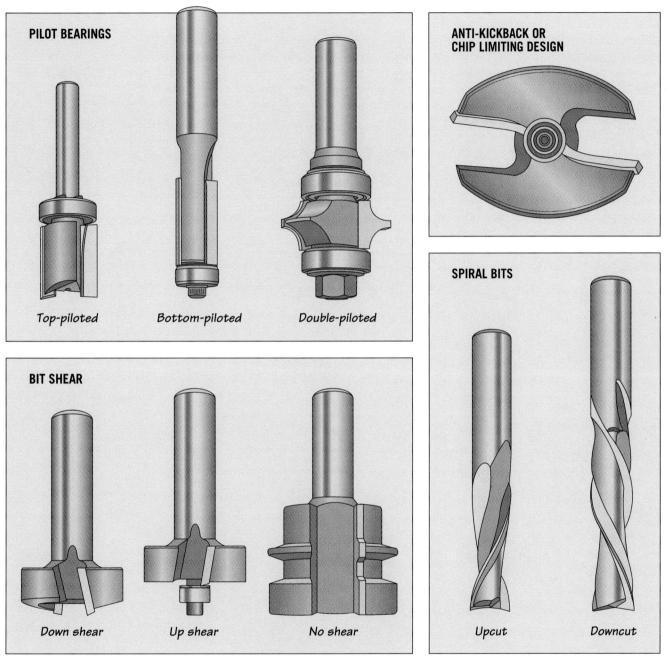

PILOT BEARINGS

Top-piloted | Bottom-piloted | Double-piloted

ANTI-KICKBACK OR CHIP LIMITING DESIGN

SPIRAL BITS

BIT SHEAR

Down shear | Up shear | No shear

Upcut | Downcut

SELECTING ROUTER BITS

• Buy the best-quality bits you can afford.

• Make sure the bit shank fits your router's collet; shanks are commmonly available in ¼- and ½-inch diameters.

• Look for bits with nonstick finishes; they reduce friction and pitch build up.

• Buy the largest bit you can find for the job at hand.

• Look for an even bond where the parts of a bit—such as the cutters and the body—meet; use a magnifying glass, if necessary.

• Buy bits with an anti-kickback design.

A SHOWCASE OF ROUTER BITS

Woodworkers use two types of router bits: edge-forming and grooving bits. A sampling of both types along with the profile each one produces in wood is illustrated at right and on the following pages. Edge-forming bits are generally used for decorative purposes, such as the bowl-edge forming bit, which is commonly used to round over kitchen countertops to prevent spills from dripping off the surface. Grooving bits, such as mortising or straight bits, are designed to plunge into a workpiece.

Certain bits from both categories are too large to be used safely in a hand-held router. These cutters are best reserved for router-table work, and are shown starting on page 30.

A hex wrench tightens the pilot bearing of the rabbeting bit shown above. Depending on the diameter of the bearing installed on the cutter, the bit can plow a rabbet up to ½ inch wide.

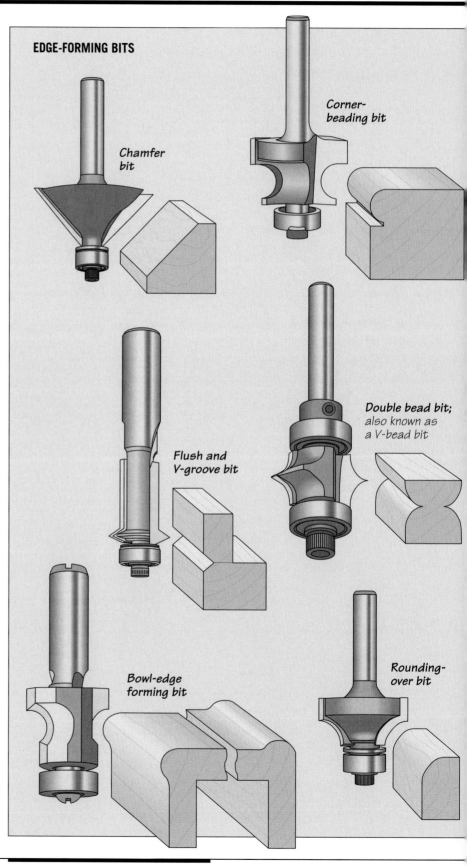

EDGE-FORMING BITS

Chamfer bit

Corner-beading bit

Flush and V-groove bit

Double bead bit; also known as a V-bead bit

Bowl-edge forming bit

Rounding-over bit

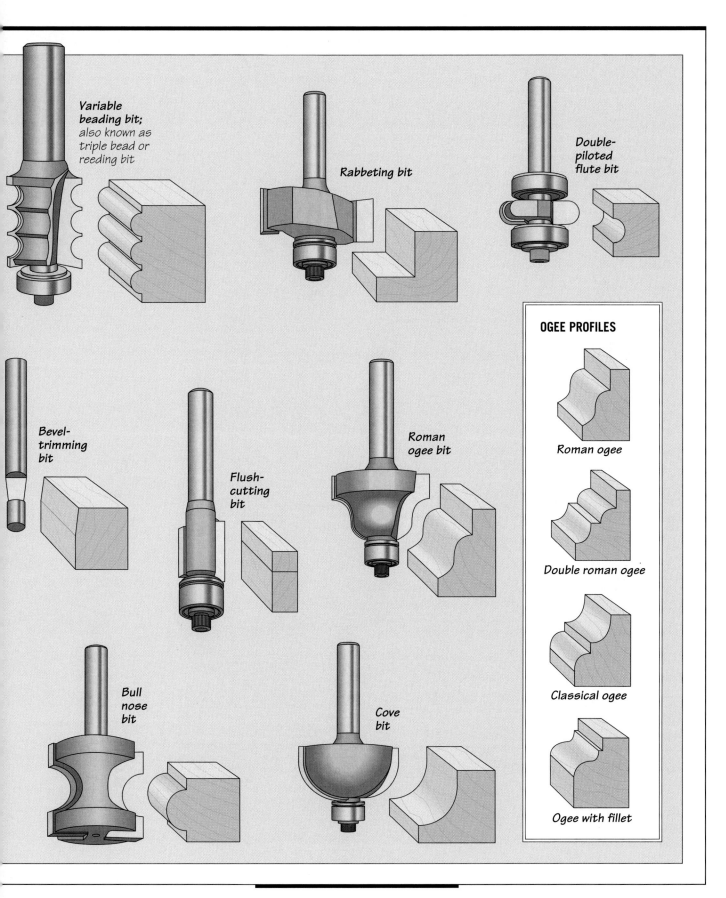

Variable beading bit; also known as triple bead or reeding bit

Rabbeting bit

Double-piloted flute bit

Bevel-trimming bit

Flush-cutting bit

Roman ogee bit

Bull nose bit

Cove bit

OGEE PROFILES

Roman ogee

Double roman ogee

Classical ogee

Ogee with fillet

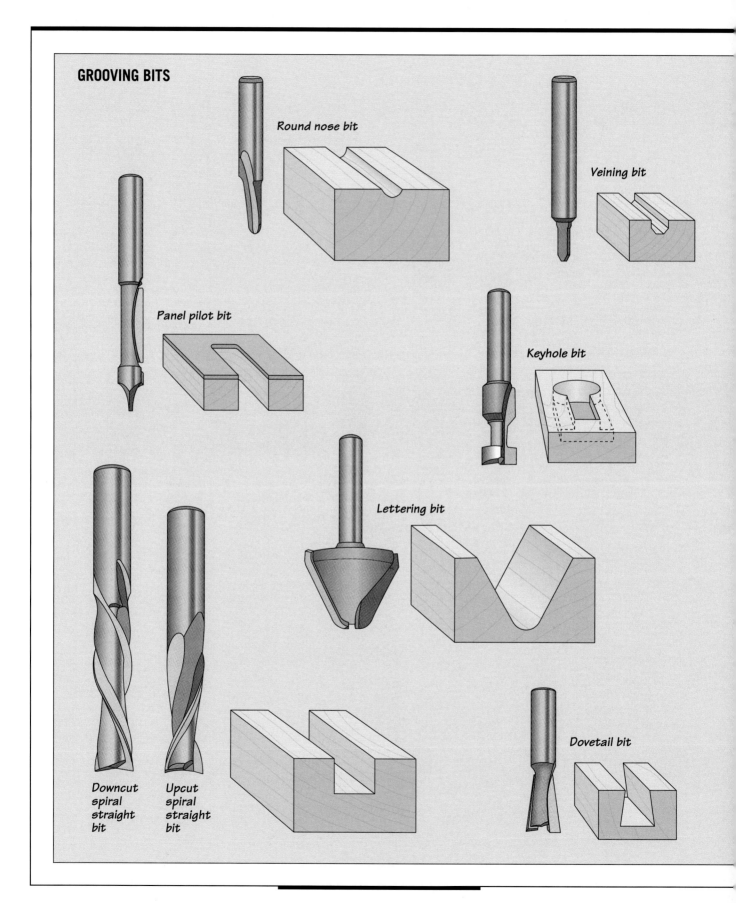

GROOVING BITS

Round nose bit

Veining bit

Panel pilot bit

Keyhole bit

Lettering bit

Downcut spiral straight bit

Upcut spiral straight bit

Dovetail bit

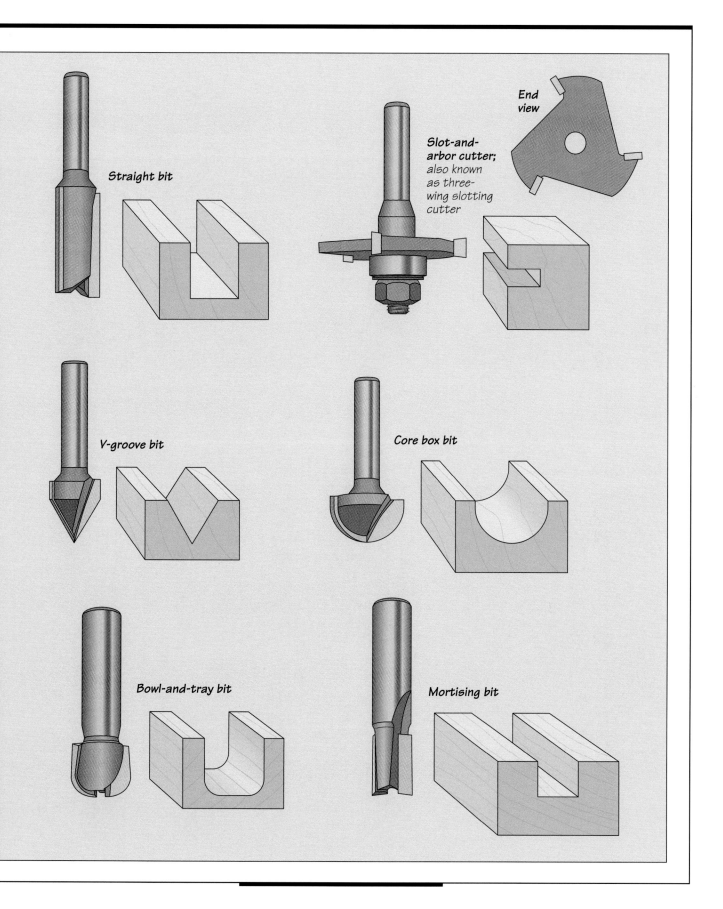

Straight bit

Slot-and-arbor cutter; also known as three-wing slotting cutter

End view

V-groove bit

Core box bit

Bowl-and-tray bit

Mortising bit

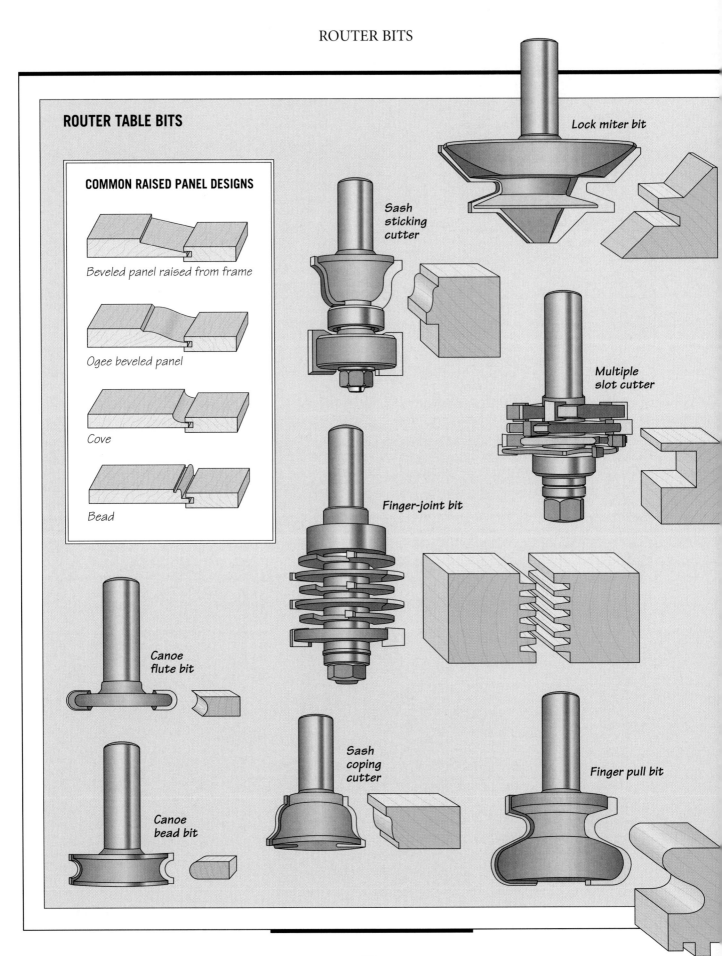

ROUTER TABLE BITS

COMMON RAISED PANEL DESIGNS

Beveled panel raised from frame

Ogee beveled panel

Cove

Bead

Lock miter bit

Sash sticking cutter

Multiple slot cutter

Finger-joint bit

Canoe flute bit

Canoe bead bit

Sash coping cutter

Finger pull bit

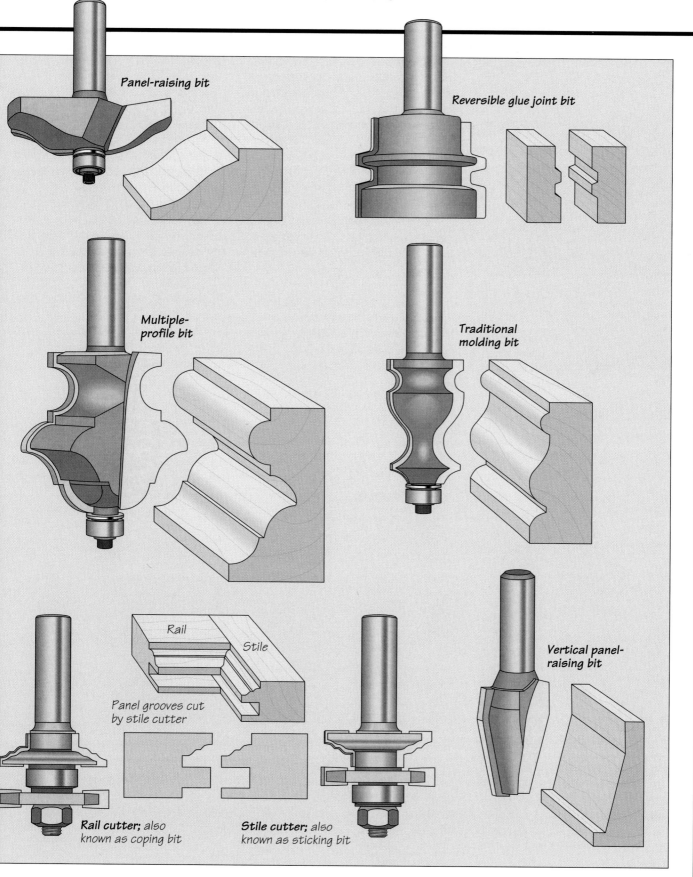

Panel-raising bit

Reversible glue joint bit

Multiple-profile bit

Traditional molding bit

Rail

Stile

Panel grooves cut by stile cutter

Vertical panel-raising bit

Rail cutter; also known as coping bit

Stile cutter; also known as sticking bit

SHARPENING AND MAINTAINING BITS

Router bits require proper care. A cutter with excessive or uneven wear will perform poorly and can even be dangerous; it will tear at wood rather than cutting it cleanly, and can even pull the router out of your hands. A dirty or dull-edged bit can overheat, causing the bit to fracture.

Get in the habit of inspecting your bits periodically for damage, wear, and built-up dirt and pitch; use a magnifying glass, if necessary. A badly damaged bit should be discarded. As shown in the

A bit is being cleaned with commercial oven cleaner. For stubborn pitch and gum, the bit can be soaked in the cleaner in a shallow pan and scrubbed with a toothbrush.

photo at left, all you need to keep cutters clean is a toothbrush along with a cleaning agent, like turpentine, a mixture of hot water and ammonia, or commercial oven cleaner.

While most bit manufacturers suggest that their products be sharpened by professionals, the job can often be done in the shop. As shown below, a bit with a properly sharpened edge can be maintained with an occasional honing. For best results with carbide cutting edges, use a diamond sharpening file. For high-speed steel bits, a benchstone is adequate.

There are times, however, when you should send out your bits to a professional sharpening service, particularly if the cutters have chipped edges or have lost their temper as a result of overheating.

SHARPENING ROUTER BITS

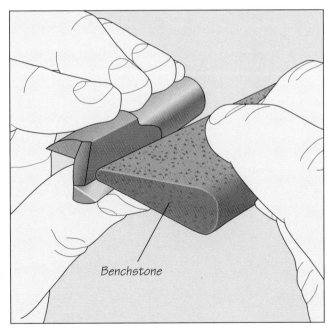

Benchstone

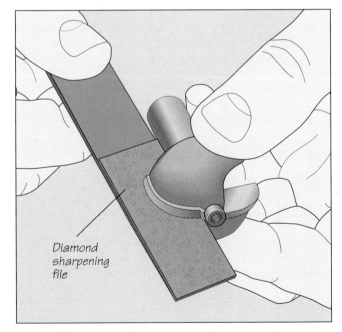

Diamond sharpening file

Sharpening a non-piloted router bit
Use a benchstone to hone the inside faces of the cutting edges of a high-speed steel bit, like the one shown above. Holding the inside face of one cutting edge flat against the abrasive surface, rub it back and forth. Repeat with the other edge. Hone both faces equally to maintain the balance of the bit.

Sharpening a piloted bit
Remove the pilot bearing *(page 26)*, then sharpen the bit as you would a non-piloted bit *(page 32)*. For a carbide-tipped cutter like the one shown above, use a diamond sharpening file. Reinstall the bearing. If it does not rotate smoothly, spray a little bearing lubricant on it. If the bearing is worn out or damaged, replace it.

A STORAGE RACK FOR BITS

The cutting edges of router bits, particularly those made of carbide, can be nicked if they are thrown together in storage. Protect your bits with a simple shop-made rack. Make the rack with your table saw, cutting four stepped rabbets along the edges of a 4-inch-thick and 8-inch-wide board that is long enough to accommodate all your bits. Outline the two outside rabbets on one end of the board so the width of each rabbet is about one-fifth the board width. The rabbet depth should be about two-thirds the stock thickness. Cut the rabbet shoulders with the stock face-down on the saw table and the edge riding along the rip fence. Use a featherboard to support the stock as you cut the rabbet cheeks. Shim the featherboard with a board set on edge and brace it with a support board so that it will press against the middle of the workpiece and minimize wobbling. Once you have cut the two outside rabbets, outline the two inside ones, making them the same width as the first two, but only one-half as deep. Saw the rabbet shoulders first, then cut the cheeks, feeding the bottom face of the stock along the fence, with the edge flat on the table *(right, above)*. Then drill a series of holes the size of the bit shanks on the rabbeted face of the rack to hold the cutters *(right, below)*.

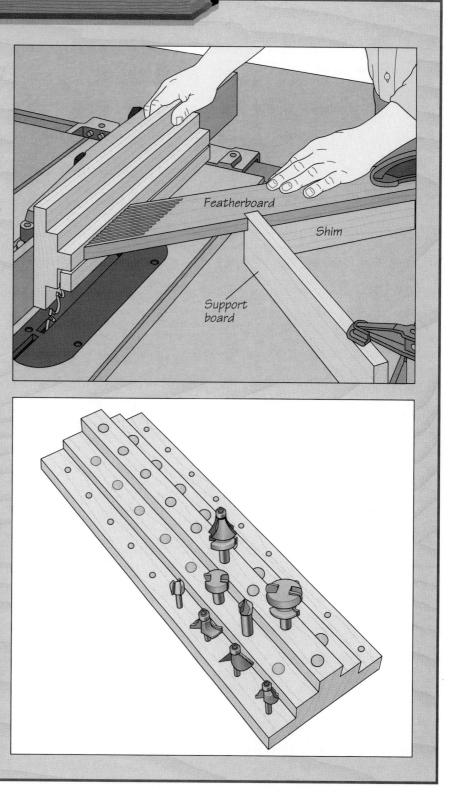

Featherboard

Shim

Support board

ROUTER TABLES

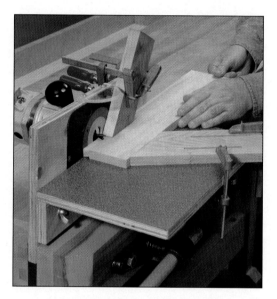

Mounted parallel to the tabletop, the vise-mounted router table shown above cuts one side of a sliding dovetail. Instructions for building this jig are on page 59.

The router table does for the router what a saw table accomplishes for the circular saw blade. It transforms a portable tool into a stationary one—and in the case of the router, enables it to perform tasks that can normally be managed only with an expensive shaper.

Mounted upside down and fixed in position, the table-mounted router allows the operator to use both hands to feed a workpiece into the bit, producing safer, more consistent results. And because stock also can be guided along a fence, or by a miter gauge, a template, or a jig, table cuts can be executed with more precision. Another benefit of the router table is that larger cutters, like those shown starting on page 30, can be used. Such bits would be dangerous and virtually impossible to control in a hand-held tool.

Although there are several makes and models of router tables on the market—and a range of accessories to spruce them up *(page 36)*—this chapter will show you how to build one in your shop. The table illustrated on page 38 is as sturdy and versatile as any commercial version, and it is simple and inexpensive to build, using readily available materials.

The heart of the router table is its top. A good choice is ³/4- or 1-inch-thick medium density fiberboard (MDF) sandwiched between two sheets of plastic laminate. You can also use good-quality hardwood plywood, but what you gain in strength, you may sacrifice in stability and convenience. You must select a perfectly flat, unwarped panel. And, given the dimensions commonly available for plywood, be prepared to glue two sheets face to face to create a top of adequate thickness. As shown on page 41, the top can be hinged to the leg structure, enabling it to be lifted for easy access to the router when it comes time to change bits or adjust cutting depth.

One of the most useful features of a router table—the fence—can be built from plywood and scrap lumber *(page 44)*. For feeding stock, you can use either a miter gauge that rides in a slot in the top *(page 46)* or one that is guided along the edges of the table *(page 48)*. A shop-made router table can also incorporate all of the essential safety features normally found on commercial models, including remote on/off switches, dust collection hoods, and bit guards. Instructions for adding each of these elements to the basic table design are presented starting on page 49.

In addition to basic edge-forming, a shop-made table is tailor-made for performing complex routing and shaping operations. The chapter shows a range of useful router-table cuts, from stopped grooves *(page 53)* and a raised arched panel *(page 54)* to a cope-and-stick joint *(page 57)*.

The curved top of the arched panel shown at left is being beveled on a table-mounted router fitted with a vertical panel-raising bit. A two-piece jig clamped to the fence has an identical curve cut into it, helping the operator feed the workpiece evenly. The featherboard holding the panel against the fence has been clamped to a thick shim to apply pressure high up on the workpiece, minimizing wobbling.

COMMERCIAL ROUTER TABLES & ACCESSORIES

There is no shortage of after-market devices for router tables. A selection of the more useful ones is illustrated below and on page 37. Some items, like the speed control or remote switch, must be purchased. Others, such as fences or table inserts, can easily be fashioned in the shop for a fraction of the cost of their commercial counterparts. One advantage of most commercial router table fences is their cast-aluminum construction, which makes them strong, but lighter than the average wooden shop-made version. Better commercial fences also feature a wooden face that can be trued on the jointer (page 45). Although most of these fences come with a built-in vacuum pick up, you can add this feature to a shop-built fence, as shown on page 50.

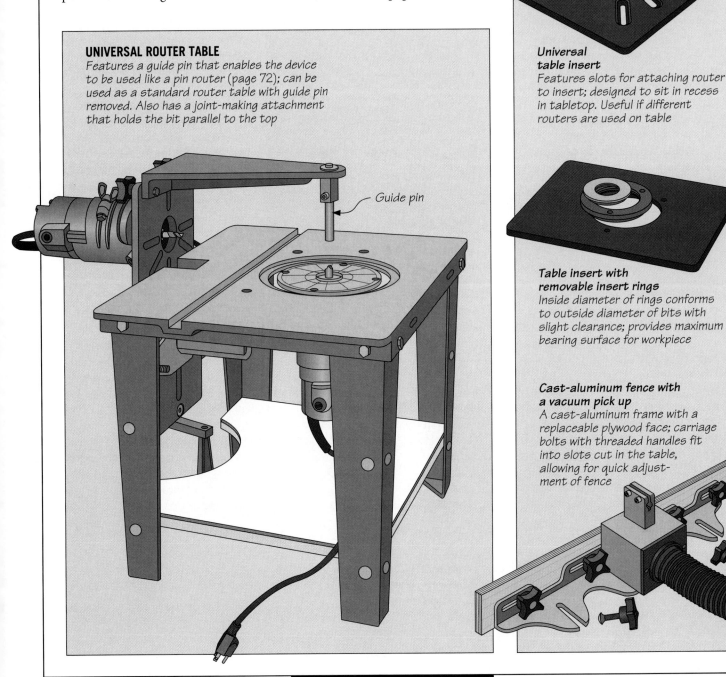

UNIVERSAL ROUTER TABLE
Features a guide pin that enables the device to be used like a pin router (page 72); can be used as a standard router table with guide pin removed. Also has a joint-making attachment that holds the bit parallel to the top

Guide pin

ROUTER ACCESSORIES

Universal table insert
Features slots for attaching router to insert; designed to sit in recess in tabletop. Useful if different routers are used on table

Table insert with removable insert rings
Inside diameter of rings conforms to outside diameter of bits with slight clearance; provides maximum bearing surface for workpiece

Cast-aluminum fence with a vacuum pick up
A cast-aluminum frame with a replaceable plywood face; carriage bolts with threaded handles fit into slots cut in the table, allowing for quick adjustment of fence

The router table shown at right can be bolted to a saw table, as in the illustration; it is also available with legs for a freestanding setup. The top is made of cast-iron, making it as sturdy and flat as the saw table.

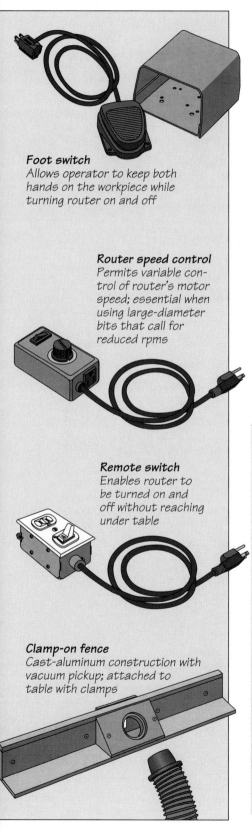

Foot switch
Allows operator to keep both hands on the workpiece while turning router on and off

Router speed control
Permits variable control of router's motor speed; essential when using large-diameter bits that call for reduced rpms

Remote switch
Enables router to be turned on and off without reaching under table

Clamp-on fence
Cast-aluminum construction with vacuum pickup; attached to table with clamps

SHOP TIP

Shop-made router table insert
To make your own insert for a router table, use a piece of ¼- or ⅜-inch-thick acrylic (polycarbonate or phenolic resin) cut to fit in the table opening. (For a shop-built table, refer to page 42 for instructions on cutting an opening in the top.) To drill a bit clearance hole through the insert, mark the center of the surface by drawing two intersecting lines on it from corner to corner. Then clamp the insert to your drill press table, placing a backup panel under the insert and centering the surface under a hole saw—which should be slightly larger than the largest router bit you plan to use.

A SHOP-BUILT ROUTER TABLE

ANATOMY OF A SHOP-BUILT ROUTER TABLE

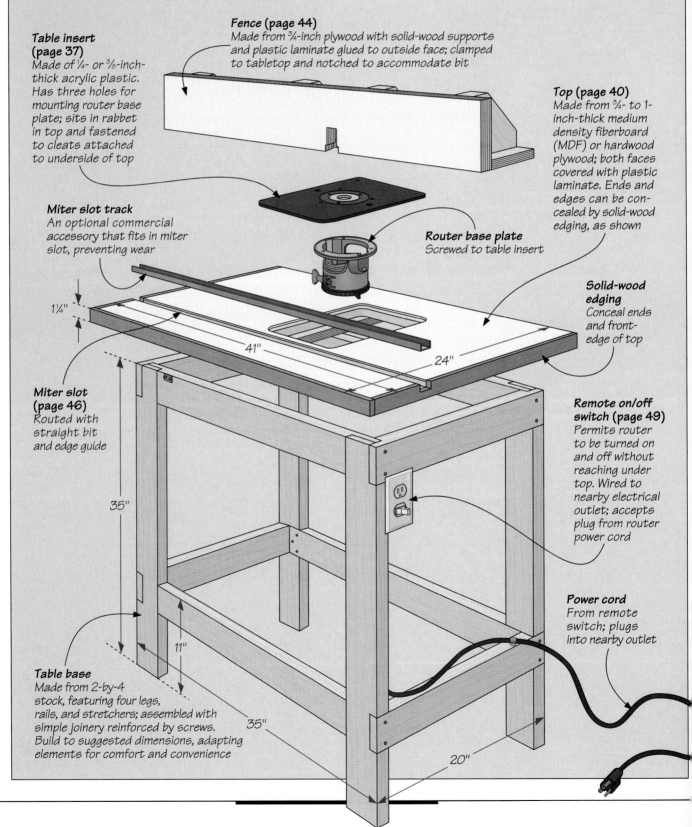

Table insert (page 37)
Made of ¼- or ⅜-inch-thick acrylic plastic. Has three holes for mounting router base plate; sits in rabbet in top and fastened to cleats attached to underside of top

Fence (page 44)
Made from ¾-inch plywood with solid-wood supports and plastic laminate glued to outside face; clamped to tabletop and notched to accommodate bit

Top (page 40)
Made from ¾- to 1-inch-thick medium density fiberboard (MDF) or hardwood plywood; both faces covered with plastic laminate. Ends and edges can be concealed by solid-wood edging, as shown

Miter slot track
An optional commercial accessory that fits in miter slot, preventing wear

Router base plate
Screwed to table insert

Solid-wood edging
Conceal ends and front-edge of top

Miter slot (page 46)
Routed with straight bit and edge guide

Remote on/off switch (page 49)
Permits router to be turned on and off without reaching under top. Wired to nearby electrical outlet; accepts plug from router power cord

Power cord
From remote switch; plugs into nearby outlet

Table base
Made from 2-by-4 stock, featuring four legs, rails, and stretchers; assembled with simple joinery reinforced by screws. Build to suggested dimensions, adapting elements for comfort and convenience

1¼"

41"

24"

35"

11"

35"

20"

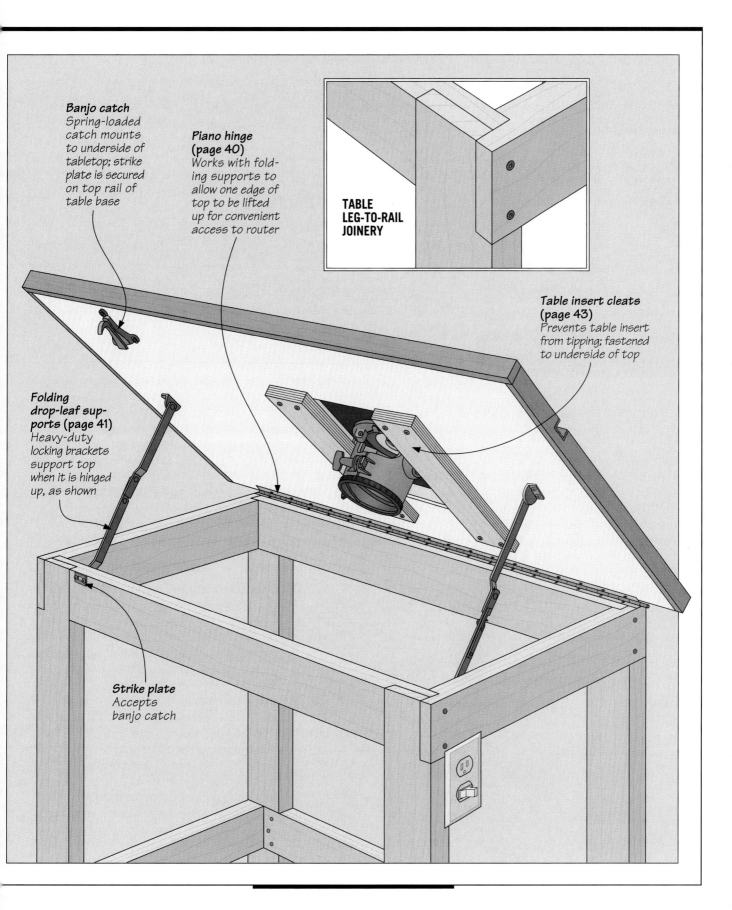

Banjo catch
Spring-loaded catch mounts to underside of tabletop; strike plate is secured on top rail of table base

Piano hinge (page 40)
Works with folding supports to allow one edge of top to be lifted up for convenient access to router

TABLE LEG-TO-RAIL JOINERY

Table insert cleats (page 43)
Prevents table insert from tipping; fastened to underside of top

Folding drop-leaf supports (page 41)
Heavy-duty locking brackets support top when it is hinged up, as shown

Strike plate
Accepts banjo catch

BUILDING A ROUTER TABLE

Once plastic laminate has been glued down to a router tabletop, as shown at right, and the adhesive has cured, a laminate trimmer can be used to cut the excess flush with the ends and edges of the top (above). Durable, scratch-resistant, and slick, the plastic should be applied to both sides of the top to minimize the risk of warping as a result of humidity changes.

ASSEMBLING THE FRAME AND ADDING THE TOP

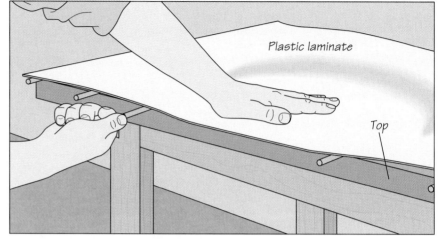

1 Gluing the plastic laminate to the top

Start the project by building the leg-and-rail assembly, referring to the anatomy illustrations on pages 38 and 39 for suggested dimensions and joinery. Then, cut the top to size and set it on the assembly. Cut two sheets of ⅛-inch plastic laminate a few inches larger than the top. Working outdoors, or in a well-ventilated area indoors, apply contact cement to one side of the top and one of the plastic sheets. Let the adhesive dry following the manufacturer's directions. Since it will be impossible to reposition the plastic once it contacts the top, use the method shown above to bond the laminate in place. Place several ¼-inch dowels at equal intervals across the top, then set the plastic on the dowels, centering it on the top—without contacting it. Pull out the middle dowel and press the plastic down with your free hand. Continue in this fashion, removing the dowels and pressing the laminate down, until the entire sheet contacts the surface. Flatten the plastic with a hand roller, then trim the excess flush with the top *(photo, left)*. Repeat the process on the top's other side. Glue solid-wood edging to the ends and front edge of the top.

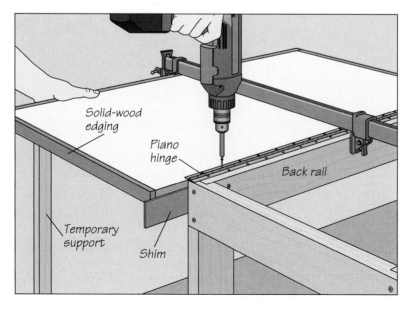

2 Attaching the hinge to the top and leg assembly

Fasten the back edge of the top to the table's leg assembly using a piano hinge. Start by positioning one hinge leaf on the top edge of the assembly's back rail so the hinge cylinder just hangs over the rail and mark the locations of the screw holes. Then drill pilot holes at the marks, reposition the hinge and drive the screws. To fasten the other leaf to the top, you will need to hold the top at the correct distance from the back rail with its underside level with the top edge of the rail. Clamp the top to the leg assembly, separating the two pieces with a shim the same thickness as the hinge cylinder diameter—typically ³⁄₃₂ inch. Cut two boards the same length as the legs and use them to support the far edge of the top. Then with the free hinge leaf flat on the top, mark the locations for the screws, bore pilot holes, and drive in the screws *(left)*.

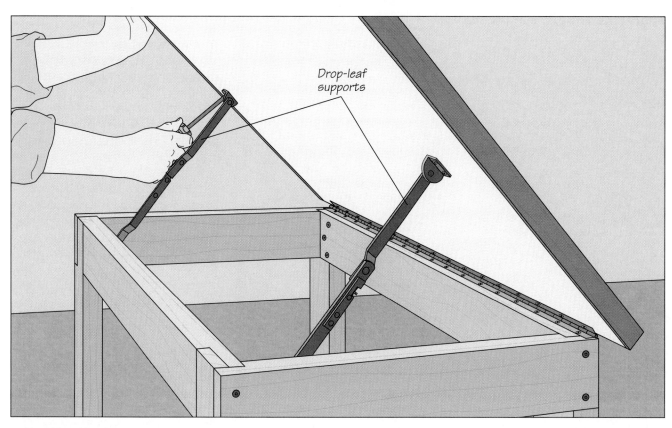

3 Installing the support brackets
Use two locking drop-leaf supports to hold up the top when you need to access the router. Brace the top open at a 45° angle, extend one of the supports, and position it with one end on the underside of the top and the other end on the inside face of the side rail near the corner. Mark the screw holes and drill pilot holes at the marks, then reposition the support and drive the screws. Repeat to install the other support *(above)*.

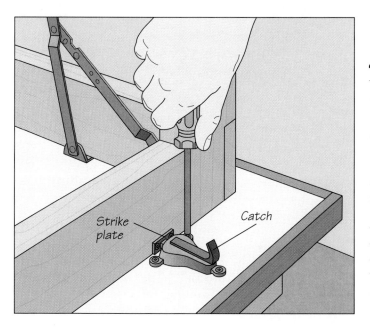

4 Installing the catch
Use a spring-loaded catch to secure the front edge of the top to the front rail of the leg assembly when the router table is in use. For the banjo catch shown in the illustration at left, set the table upside down on a work surface and position the catch on the underside of the top so the bolt is about ⅛ inch from the rail when it is retracted. Mark the screw holes, then engage the strike plate with the bolt. Extend the bolt, hold the strike plate flush against the rail, and mark its screw holes and bolt opening on the rail. Use a chisel to cut the bolt opening recess in the rail and an electric drill to bore pilot holes at the screw hole marks. Then fasten the strike plate to the rail and the catch to the top. To lift the top, simply retract the bolt; when you lower the top onto the rails, the bolt will automatically engage the strike plate.

PREPARING THE TOP FOR THE ROUTER

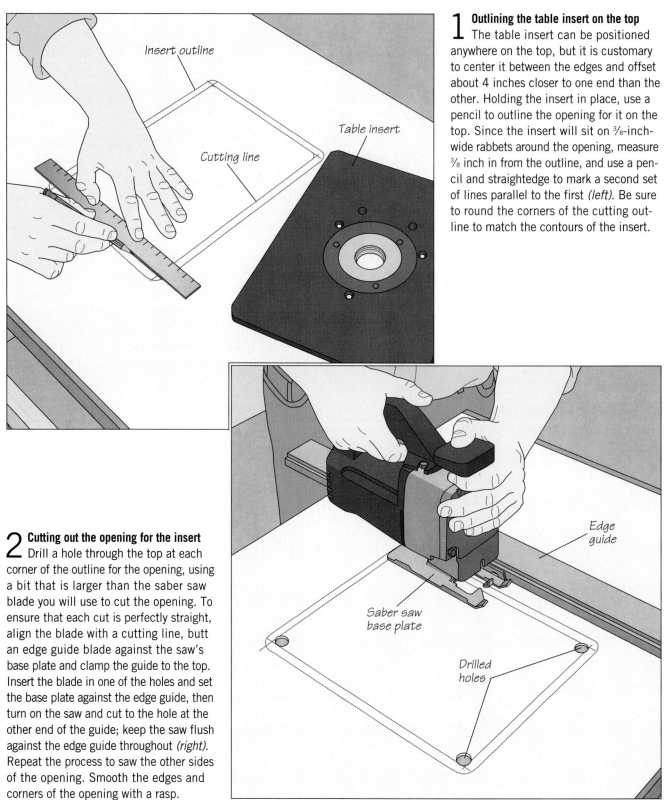

Insert outline

Cutting line

Table insert

Edge guide

Saber saw base plate

Drilled holes

1 **Outlining the table insert on the top**
The table insert can be positioned anywhere on the top, but it is customary to center it between the edges and offset about 4 inches closer to one end than the other. Holding the insert in place, use a pencil to outline the opening for it on the top. Since the insert will sit on ⅜-inch-wide rabbets around the opening, measure ⅜ inch in from the outline, and use a pencil and straightedge to mark a second set of lines parallel to the first *(left)*. Be sure to round the corners of the cutting outline to match the contours of the insert.

2 **Cutting out the opening for the insert**
Drill a hole through the top at each corner of the outline for the opening, using a bit that is larger than the saber saw blade you will use to cut the opening. To ensure that each cut is perfectly straight, align the blade with a cutting line, butt an edge guide blade against the saw's base plate and clamp the guide to the top. Insert the blade in one of the holes and set the base plate against the edge guide, then turn on the saw and cut to the hole at the other end of the guide; keep the saw flush against the edge guide throughout *(right)*. Repeat the process to saw the other sides of the opening. Smooth the edges and corners of the opening with a rasp.

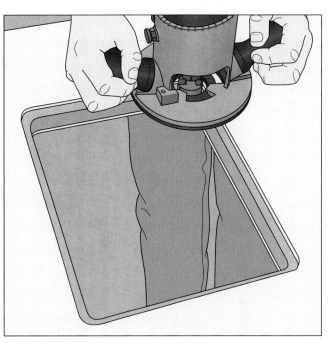

3 **Routing the ledge**
Install a ⅜-inch piloted rabbeting bit in your router and set the cutting height to the thickness of the table insert *(above, left)*. If the insert is thicker than ¼ inch, adjust the bit height to one-half the insert thickness and rout the ledge in two passes. To make the cut, hold the router base plate flat on the top with the bit inside the opening but clear of the stock. Turn on the tool and ease the bit into an edge of the opening until the pilot bearing contacts the stock. Then guide the router around the opening *(above, right)*, stopping the cut when you return to your starting point. Sand the ledge smooth, then test-fit the table insert in the opening. It should be perfectly flush with the top; if it protrudes, increase the router's cutting depth slightly and repeat the cut.

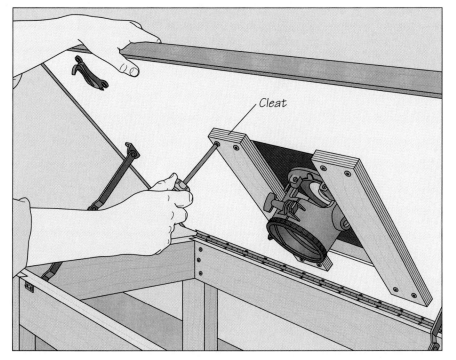

Cleat

4 **Securing the table insert to the top**
Because the top is hinged, it is a good idea to anchor the table insert in place to prevent it from toppling onto the shop floor —along with your router—when the top is lifted. Position the table insert in its opening—with the router base plate attached —then cut two ¾-inch plywood cleats 3 inches wide and a few inches longer than the width of the table opening. Position the cleats so they overlap the ends of the opening by about 1 inch and fasten them to the underside of the top *(left)*. Then drill two countersunk holes through the insert —one into each cleat—and drive a screw into each hole. Make sure the screw heads lie level with or slightly below the top surface of the table insert.

MAKING A FENCE

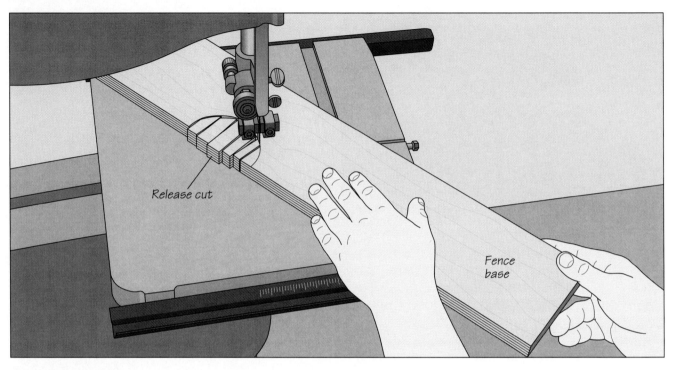

Release cut

Fence base

1 Preparing the pieces

Cut the fence base and upright from ¾-inch plywood, making the pieces as long as the top. Then cut four triangular supports from 1-inch-thick solid stock. Each support should have one 90° angle to fit in the corner between the base and upright; trim the other two angles so they will not extend beyond the edges of the base and upright when the fence is assembled. To prepare the base, position it on the table and outline a 2½-inch-diameter arc on one edge, centered on the bit clearance hole in the table insert. Cut the arc on your band saw, making a series of release cuts through the waste from the edge to the cutting line. Then saw along the cutting line *(above)*, feeding the base across the saw table with both hands. Prepare the upright the same way, but cut a square opening on the bottom edge just wide and high enough to accommodate the largest bit you plan to use on the table.

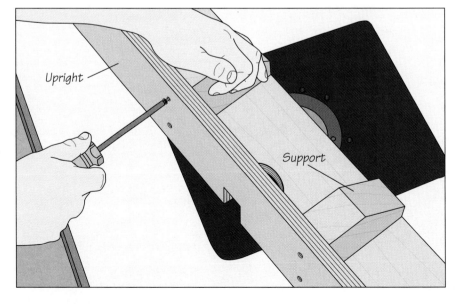

Upright

Support

2 Assembling the fence

Attach the fence base and upright together with glue and screws, using a try square to keep the pieces at right angles. Next, attach the supports in place *(right)*; they will help ensure that the base and upright remain perpendicular to each other. Position the supports adjoining the fence opening to accommodate any dust extraction hood you plan to install on the fence *(page 50)*.

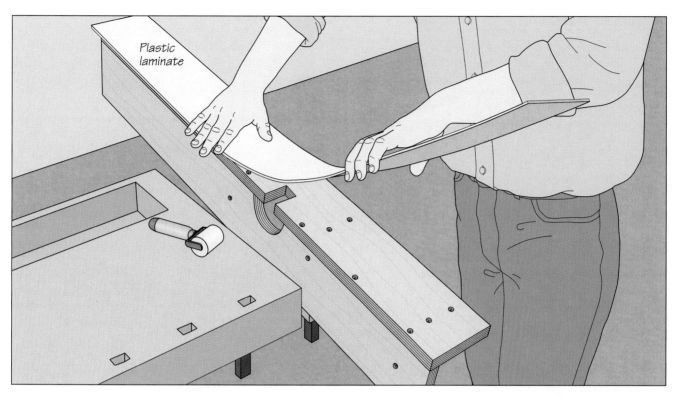

Plastic laminate

3 Finishing the fence

To help your stock slide more easily along the fence, glue a piece of plastic laminate to the outside face of the upright. Secure the base in a bench vise and cut a piece of laminate slightly larger than the upright. Then fix the plastic to the fence with contact cement *(above)*, following the same procedure used to bond the laminate to the top *(page 40)*. Press the plastic down with a hand roller, then cut the excess flush with the edges and ends of the upright using a laminate trimmer.

SHOP TIP

Truing a commercial fence

A router table fence must be perpendicular to the table and its upright portion must be perfectly flat. Not all commercial fences meet these requirements. If the fence upright is faced with wood, you can square it on your jointer. Set the machine for a very shallow cut and feed the fence into the cutterhead, pressing the upright flat on the tables and the base flush against the jointer fence. Check the fence with a try square and make another pass, if necessary. **Caution:** Make sure any screws in the router fence upright are recessed well below the surface.

ROUTING A MITER SLOT

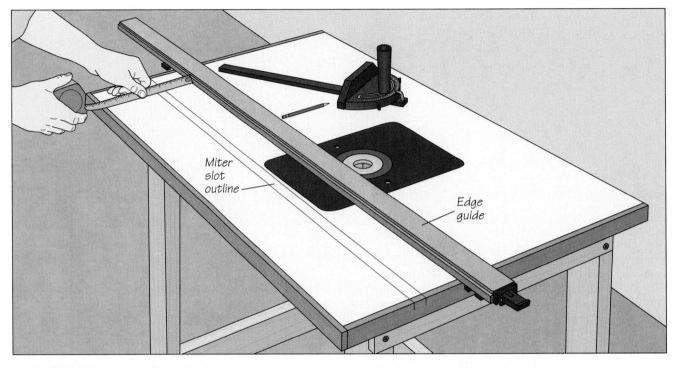

Miter
slot
outline

Edge
guide

1 Outlining the slot and setting up the cut
Position your miter gauge on the router table with
its bar parallel to the table's edges and a gap of at least
½ inch between the bar and table insert. Mark the edges
of the bar on the top, then extend the marks along the
table's length, using a carpenter's square and a straightedge to ensure that the lines remain parallel to the
table's edges. Next, install a straight bit in your router
the same diameter as the width of the miter bar. Measure
the distance between the bit and the edge of the router
base plate, then use the measurement to position the
straightedge that will guide your router as it plows the
miter slot *(above)*. Make sure the edge guide is parallel
to the slot outline.

2 Routing the slot
Cut the miter slot in two passes. For the first one, adjust
the router's cutting depth to one-half the thickness of the
bar—a commercial table saw miter gauge bar is typically ⅜
inch thick. With the bit clear of the table at one end, butt
the router's base plate against the edge guide and confirm
that the bit is centered between the layout lines. Then turn
on the tool and guide the bit into the top. Complete the
slot, keeping the router flush against the edge guide *(right)*.
Increase the cutting depth to slightly more than the full
thickness of the miter bar and make another pass.

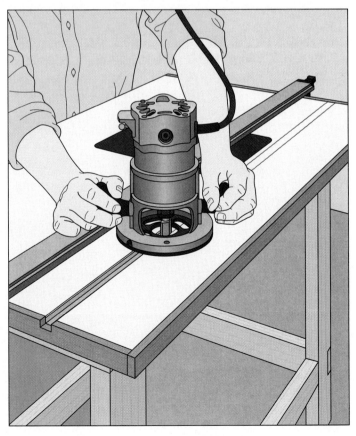

USING A MITER GAUGE

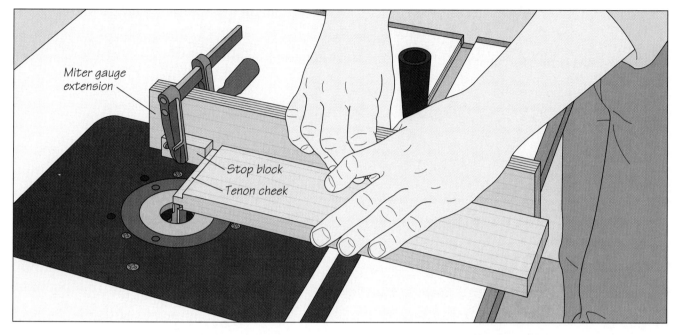

Miter gauge extension

Stop block

Tenon cheek

SHOP TIP

An aluminum miter slot track

One weakness of a router table miter slot is that repeated use will gradually wear away the sides until there is too much side-to-side play. Striking the edge of the bar with a metal punch will dimple the surface, tightening the fit, but eventually you will need to rout a new slot. A better solution is to extend the life of a miter slot by fitting it with a commercial track. Made of aluminum and sized to accommodate standard miter bars, the metal track is screwed to the base of the table slot, as shown below.

The bottom of the track is slightly concave (inset), so tightening or loosening the screws will flex or slacken the walls to fine-tune the fit of the gauge in the slot.

Routing a tenon

A miter gauge is typically used to feed stock into the bit for cuts across the grain. To rout a tenon, as shown above, start by installing a straight bit in the router and mounting the tool in the table; the diameter of the bit should equal the desired width of the tenon cheeks. Screw an extension board to the miter gauge; this will minimize tearout and increase the bearing surface of the gauge. Align the workpiece with the bit, then butt a stop block against the end of the board and clamp the block to the extension; the stop block will help ensure that all the tenons you cut will be the same length. To rout the tenon, set the workpiece flat on the table with an edge flush against the miter gauge and the end butted against the stop block. Then, holding the stock in place, feed it along with the miter gauge into the bit. Turn the workpiece over and repeat the cut (above).

ROUTER TABLE FEEDING JIG

Made entirely of ¾-inch plywood and two solid-wood scraps, the jig shown at right will enable you to make guided cross-grain cuts on your router table without a miter slot. Rather than running in a slot, the jig rides along the table's edges.

Cut the two pieces of the feeding guide from plywood, making them about 4 inches wide and as long as the width of the table plus the two arms. Glue and screw the guide pieces together in an L shape, using a try square to ensure that they are perpendicular. Then cut the arms from ¾-inch-thick solid stock, making them about 5 inches wide and 12 inches long. Attach one of the arms to the guide, driving the screws from underneath; make sure the arm is perpendicular to the guide and its outside edge is flush with the end of the guide.

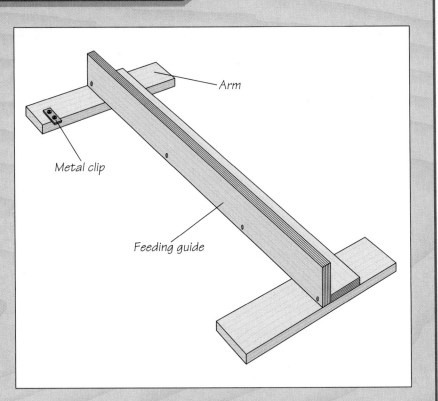

Arm

Metal clip

Feeding guide

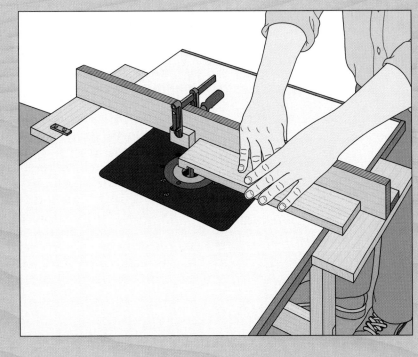

Set the jig on the router table, placing a slip of paper as a shim between the arm and the table's edge. Butt the other arm against the opposite edge and clamp it to the guide. Remove the paper shim and slide the jig back and forth along the table. If there is too much play, loosen the clamp and reposition the arm; apply paste wax to the inside edges of the arms to help it slide more easily. Then screw the remaining arm to the guide. Also attach a small metal clip to one of the arms near the front end; this will prevent the jig from tipping forward.

Use the jig as you would a miter gauge *(page 47)*, holding the workpiece flush against the guide as you feed it into the bit *(left)*.

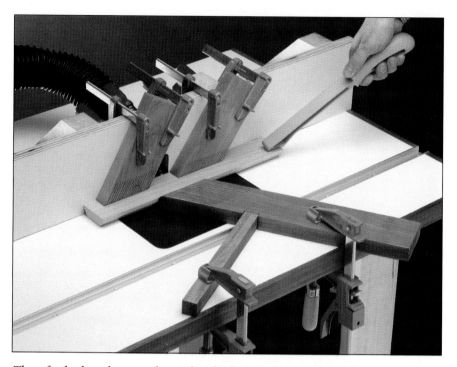

Three featherboards—two clamped to the fence and one to the table—hold the workpiece shown above safely against the fence and table while a push stick is used to feed the stock into the bit. Dust and wood chips are being extracted by a dust collection hose attached to a dust hood built into the fence.

Turning at speeds of up to 20,000 rpm, a router can be an intimidating tool—and a dangerous one, if it is used carelessly. This section will show you how to build and use several devices that can make your router table work safer.

Spinning router bits look deceptively harmless. Because their outside edges are almost invisible when the router is turning, bits can seem to be smaller than they actually are. To shield your hands from being nicked by a spinning bit, always use a bit guard that extends over the cutter. Two types—a fence-mounted guard and a freestanding version—are shown on page 51. Although you can make bit guards entirely from wood, using clear acrylic plastic or polycarbonate will allow you to view the cutting action.

The dangers of wood dust and chips are less immediate than those associated with bits, but prolonged exposure can contribute to respiratory ailments and irritate the skin and eyes. Refer to page 50 for two methods for hooking up your router table to a dust collection system in your shop.

Two of the simplest—but most important—safety devices available are shown in the photo at left. Whenever you are making a fence-guided cut on the router table, use featherboards to keep your stock pressed against the fence and table. The boards' mitered ends and flexible fingers ensure stock can only move forward, helping to prevent kickback. And to keep your hands from coming too close to a spinning bit, use a push stick to feed stock whenever possible.

SHOP TIP

Remote On/Off switch
One potential danger of router table work is reaching under the top to start and stop the router. To avoid any risk, use a remote switch to turn the tool on and off. Fasten a combination switch-receptacle to one of the table's legs. Then wire a power cord long enough to reach a nearby outlet. When you use the table, plug in the router and leave its motor switch on. Be sure to unplug the router when changing bits or adjusting the fence.

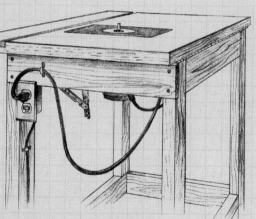

TWO DUST COLLECTION HOODS

A dust collection hood attached to your router table fence will do an efficient job of removing most of the wood dust and chips generated by the router. Two designs are illustrated on this page; both hoods surround the opening in the fence upright and are branched to a dust collection hose. The hoods are also designed so there are no gaps around the fence for air leaks that would reduce the efficiency of the dust extraction system.

The hood shown at right is made of ½-inch plywood. It has two side pieces that hug the fence supports adjoining the bit, a top flange that fits on the top edge of the fence, and a back flange that rests flush on the table. Before assembling the hood, cut a hole through the back piece for the hose. To secure the collection hose to the hood, screw an angle iron to the back piece on each side of the hole, insert the end of the hose in the hole, and use a hose clamp to fix the hose to the angle irons. Then screw the sides of the hood to the fence bracket.

You can also attach a commercial furnace duct made of sheet metal to the fence to extract dust and chips, as shown at left. In this case, space the fence supports adjoining the bit to accommodate the duct when you are building the fence *(page 44)*; the sides of the duct should fit snugly between the supports. To attach the device to the fence, cut a bracket from ½-inch plywood about 3 inches wide, including a semicircular extension that will serve as a bit guard. Use two sheet-metal screws to fasten the bracket to the duct and two wood screws to fix it to the top edge of the fence; the straight portion of the bracket's front edge should be flush with the laminated face of the fence. Secure the dust collection hose to the duct using a hose clamp.

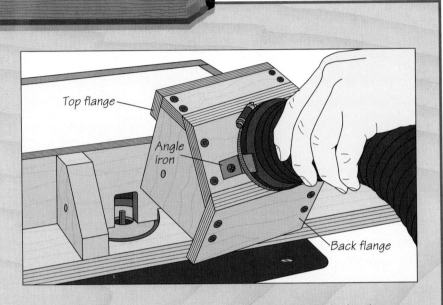

Top flange

Angle iron

Back flange

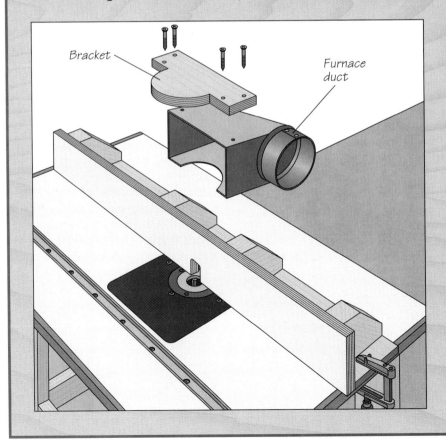

Bracket

Furnace duct

BIT GUARDS

Making and using a fence-mounted bit guard

To protect your fingers during fence-guided cuts on the router table, use a fence-mounted guard. Saw a block about 4 inches long and 3 inches wide from ¾-inch-thick stock. Then cut a semicircle of clear acrylic to the same size and screw it to the bottom edge of the block. Clamp the jig to the fence, centering it over the bit at the desired height *(right)*.

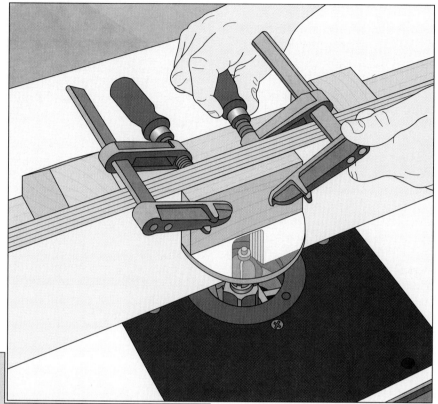

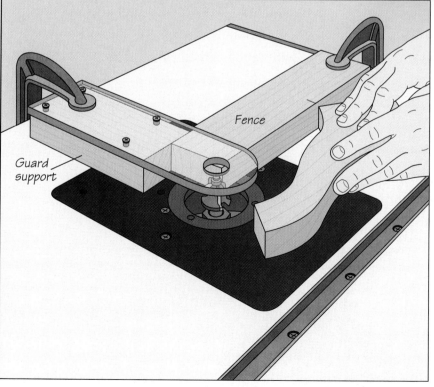

Guard
support

Fence

Freestanding bit guard

Use a freestanding bit guard like the one shown at left when you are performing freehand shaping operations. Cut a piece of clear acrylic 10 inches long and 3½ inches wide, with a semicircle at one end. Saw a support board for the guard from 1½-inch-thick stock, making it the same width, but 3 inches shorter. Screw the acrylic to the board so the ends of the pieces are flush at one end. Next, cut a fence to span from the bit to the infeed end of the table and fasten it to the front end of the support board with an angle iron, forming an L-shaped jig. To use the guard, clamp the support board and fence to the table so the bit is completely covered by the guard.

ADVANCED TABLE ROUTING

A router table's versatility is limited only by your creativity and the selection of bits in your shop. Many complex shapes and profiles can be molded on a router table by using two or more cutters in succession. As shown below, you can shape a handrail using two different bits. With a panel-raising bit *(page 54)* and a set of cope-and-stick cutters *(page 57)*, you can make an arched door panel on the router table, and then produce attractive joinery to hold the door frame together.

There are some limitations on the work you can do on a router table, most governed by the bit size. Some cutters are too large for smaller routers to handle safely. A horizontal panel-raising bit *(page 56)* that is larger than 2½ inches in diameter can only be used in a router capable of generating at least 3 horsepower. Also, when using large bits, you

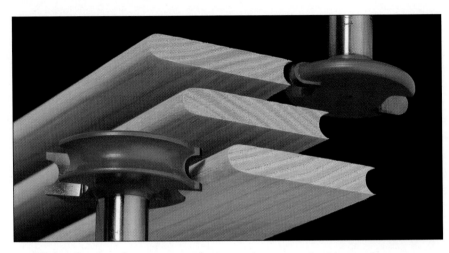

usually have to slow the router speed—a typical speed for large cutters is 8,000 rpm; refer to the manufacturer's instructions. One way to achieve comparable results with a smaller bit in a low-power router is to use a vertical panel-raising bit *(page 54)*.

Like cope-and-stick sets, the canoe bits shown above make matching cuts—in this case, flutes and beads. The canoe joint they create forms a seamless joint regardless of the angle of the boards—an essential feature in boat building.

SHAPING COMPLEX MOLDING

Forming a handrail

Start by installing a ⅜-inch round-over bit in your router and mounting the tool in the table. Use three featherboards to support the handrail blank, clamping two to the fence—one on each side of the bit—and the third to the table, raised on a shim. (In the illustrations at right, the featherboard on the outfeed side of the fence has been removed for clarity.) Position the fence for a shallow first pass—about ⅛ inch. Then feed the workpiece top face-down into the bit, keeping the stock flat on the table and flush against the fence *(right)*. Finish the pass with a push stick. Repeat the cut with the other edge against the fence, then make the second series of passes, this time with the fence aligned with the center of the bit's pilot bearing. To complete the operation, replace the round-over bit with the handrail cutter. Feeding the stock bottom face-down, make two passes on each edge *(inset)*. Start with a shallow cut, increasing to the full depth with the second pass.

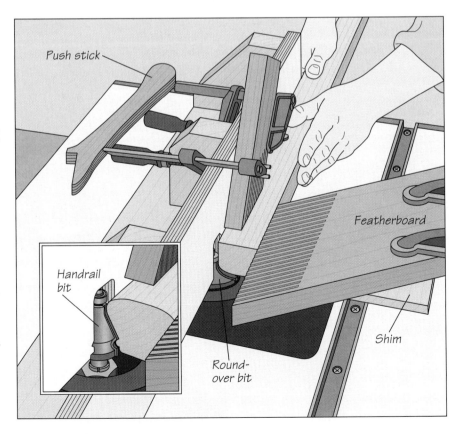

Push stick

Handrail bit

Featherboard

Round-over bit

Shim

ROUTING A STOPPED GROOVE

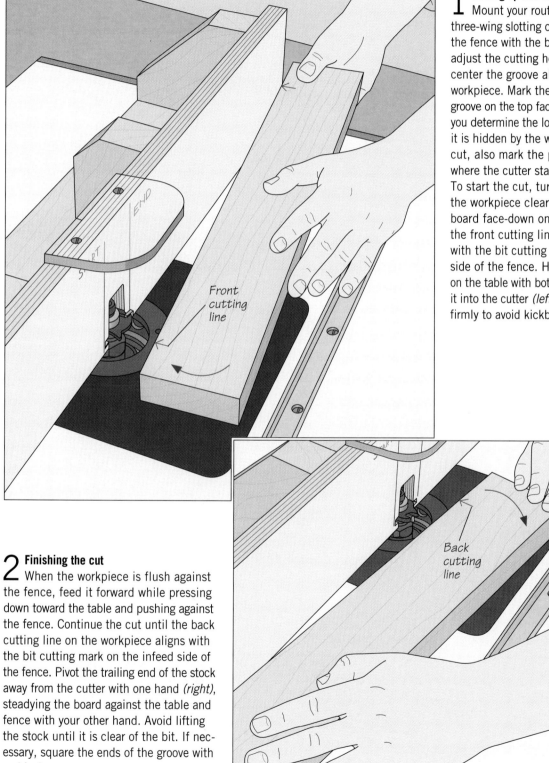

Front
cutting
line

Back
cutting
line

1 Setting up and starting the cut
Mount your router in the table with a three-wing slotting cutter in the tool. Align the fence with the bit's pilot bearing and adjust the cutting height of the cutter to center the groove along the edge of the workpiece. Mark the start and end of the groove on the top face of the stock. To help you determine the location of the bit when it is hidden by the workpiece during this cut, also mark the points on the fence where the cutter starts and stops cutting. To start the cut, turn on the router with the workpiece clear of the bit. Hold the board face-down on the table and align the front cutting line on the workpiece with the bit cutting mark on the outfeed side of the fence. Holding the board flat on the table with both hands, slowly pivot it into the cutter *(left)*. Grip the workpiece firmly to avoid kickback.

2 Finishing the cut
When the workpiece is flush against the fence, feed it forward while pressing down toward the table and pushing against the fence. Continue the cut until the back cutting line on the workpiece aligns with the bit cutting mark on the infeed side of the fence. Pivot the trailing end of the stock away from the cutter with one hand *(right)*, steadying the board against the table and fence with your other hand. Avoid lifting the stock until it is clear of the bit. If necessary, square the ends of the groove with a chisel.

RAISING AN ARCHED PANEL WITH A VERTICAL PANEL-RAISING BIT

1 Setting up the cut
Cut the panel to size on your band saw, then mount your router fitted with a vertical panel-raising bit in the table. Position the fence for a shallow cut so you can reach your final depth in two passes. To raise the arched portion of the panel, prepare a feeding jig. Using the panel as a guide, outline the desired curve on one face of a 1-inch-thick board. Then cut the curve and saw the board in two at the midpoint of the arch. Sand the cut ends smooth and screw the two pieces to the fence on each side of the bit to form a cradle in which you will be able to swivel the arched portion of the panel *(right)*. To support the panel during the cut, clamp a featherboard to the table, propping it on a thick shim so the featherboard presses the workpiece flush against the fence.

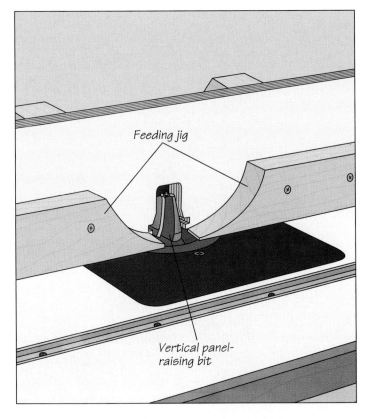

Feeding jig

Vertical panel-
raising bit

2 Starting the cut
Holding the outside face of the panel flush against the fence, slowly lower the top end onto the cutter. Tilt the bottom of the panel toward the outfeed end of the table so the workpiece contacts the bit at the start of the arched portion. With your right hand gripping the bottom corner of the panel and your left hand pressing the face against the fence, begin rotating the workpiece in a clockwise direction, swiveling the bottom end toward you *(below)*.

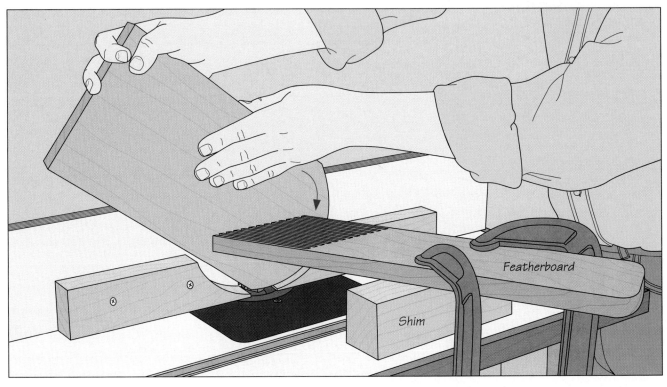

Featherboard

Shim

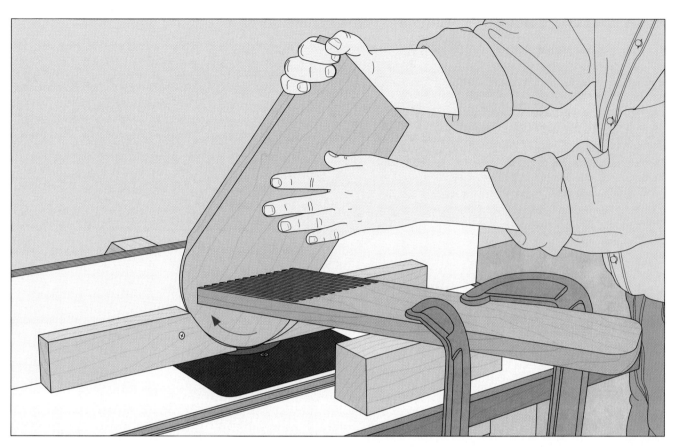

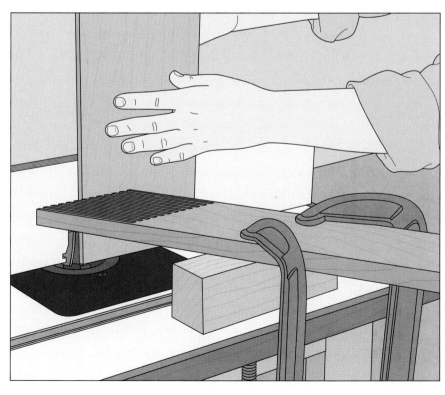

3 Finishing the cut
Continue rotating the panel toward you *(above)* until the arched section has been shaped from one end to the other. Then slowly lift the panel free of the cutter. Reposition the fence to the final cutting depth and repeat the cut.

4 Raising the sides and bottom of the panel
Unscrew the feeding jig from the fence, then position the fence to start raising the edges and straight end of the panel with a shallow pass. Feed the panel while pressing it flat against the fence *(left)*. To reduce tearout, cut the bottom of the panel first, then the sides. Back the fence away from the bit to reach your final cutting depth and make another pass on the straight end and edges.

RAISING A CURVED PANEL WITH A HORIZONTAL PANEL-RAISING BIT

1 Setting up and starting the cut
Bandsaw the panel to size, then install a horizontal panel-raising bit in your router and mount the tool in the table. Adjust the bit for a shallow cut so you can reach the final depth in two or more passes. To raise the arched portion of the panel, clamp a freestanding bit guard with a fence to the table *(page 51)*. Holding the panel flat on the table with the curved end flush against the fence, pivot the stock into the bit until the corner contacts the pilot bearing *(right)*.

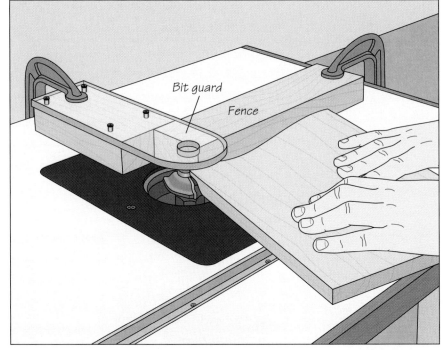

Bit guard

Fence

2 Raising the curved end of the panel
Pressing the stock against the bit's pilot bearing, feed the curved end of the panel into the bit *(below)*. Raise the cutter by no more than ⅛ inch and make another pass, continuing as necessary to reach your final depth.

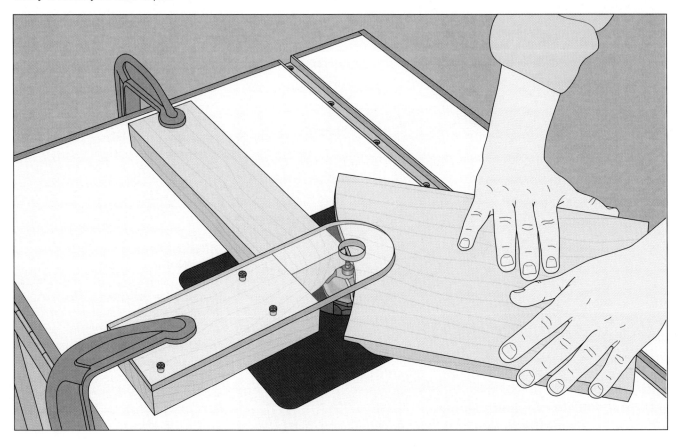

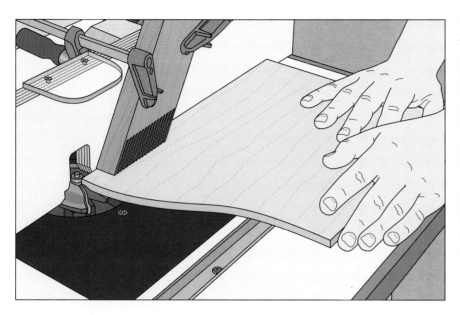

3 Raising the straight sides of the panel
Remove the freestanding bit guard and clamp a standard fence to the table, aligning its outside face with the bit's pilot bearing. Lower the bit to set a shallow cutting depth. To support the panel during the cut, secure a featherboard to the fence just to the infeed side of the cutter. Holding the workpiece flat on the table, feed it with your right hand and press it flat against the fence with your left *(left)*. Cut the bottom of the panel first, then the sides. Make as many passes as necessary, raising the bit no more than ⅛ inch at a time.

ROUTING A COPE-AND-STICK JOINT

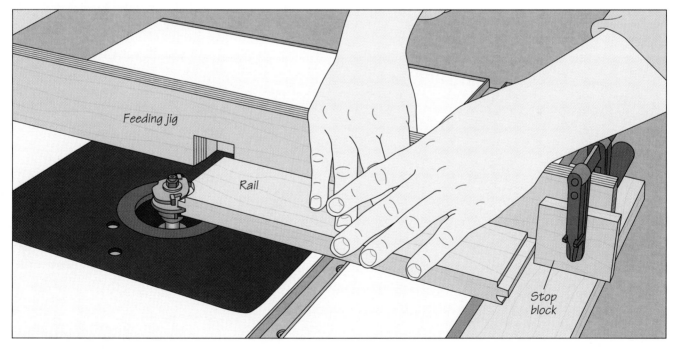

Feeding jig

Rail

Stop block

1 Cutting the tongues in the rail
Make a cope-and-stick joint by first cutting tongues in the ends of the rails, then rout the grooves for the panel along the inside edges of the rails and stiles. The grooves in the stiles will accommodate the rail tongues. For the tongues, install a piloted coping bit—or rail cutter—in your router and mount the tool in the table. Set the cutting depth by butting the end of a rail against the bit and adjusting the router's depth setting so the top of the uppermost cutter is slightly above the workpiece. Feed the stock using a jig like the one shown on page 48, cutting a notch in it to accommodate the bit and pilot bearing. Also butt a stop block against the end of the rail and clamp the block to the jig. Pressing the outside face of the stock flat on the table, hold the rail flush against the jig and stop block throughout each cut *(above)*.

2 Adjusting the sticking bit

Replace the coping bit with a piloted sticking bit—also known as a stile cutter. To set the cutting depth, butt the end of a completed rail against the bit and raise or lower the bit so that the groove-cutting teeth are level with the rail tongue *(right)*. Align the fence with the edge of the pilot bearing.

3 Cutting the grooves

Use three featherboards to secure the workpiece during each cut. Clamp one to the table opposite the bit and the other two to the fence on either side of the cutter. (In the illustration below, the featherboard on the outfeed side of the fence has been removed for clarity). Make each cut holding the stock's outside face down, pressing the workpiece against the fence. Use a push stick to complete the pass.

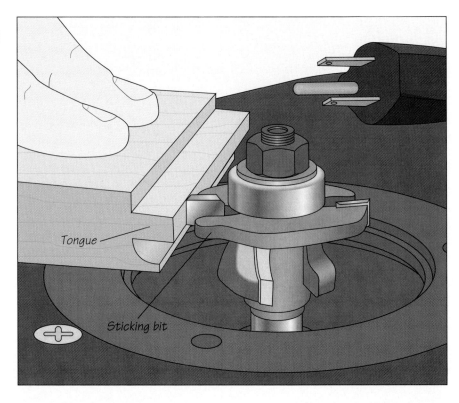

Tongue

Sticking bit

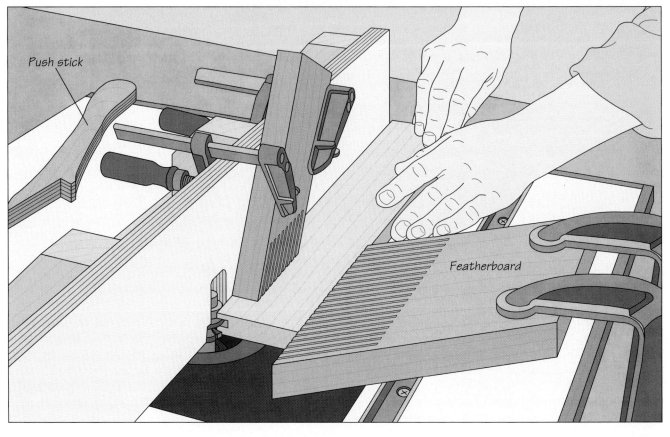

Push stick

Featherboard

VISE-MOUNTED ROUTER TABLE

The jig shown at right, made entirely of ¾-inch plywood, is simpler to build than a full-size router table and has the added benefit of holding the router horizontally—a useful feature for many operations, such as cutting joints or raising panels. Refer to the illustration for suggested dimensions.

Screw the table support to the table, forming an L, then prepare the fence. Start by cutting an opening through it with rabbets to accommodate a table insert *(page 42)*, then drill two holes through the fence for carriage bolts, one near each end. With a straight bit in a router, lengthen the hole on the outfeed side of the fence into a curved slot. Fasten the adjustable end of the table support to the fence with a carriage bolt, washer, and a wing nut. Bolt the infeed side just loosely enough for the table to be able to pivot when the other end is raised or lowered.

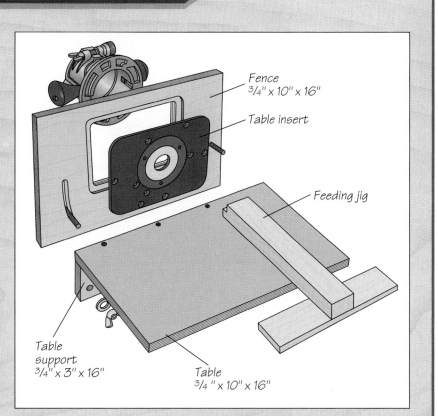

Fence
¾" x 10" x 16"

Table insert

Feeding jig

Table support
¾" x 3" x 16"

Table
¾" x 10" x 16"

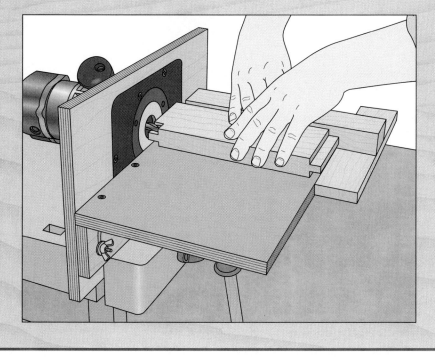

To use the jig, fasten the table insert to the fence, attach the router to the insert, and secure the fence in a vise. To rout a tenon, as shown at left, make a feeding jig *(page 48)*, using only one board to ride along the edge of the table. Then set the workpiece face down on the table, butting its edge against the bit. Loosen the wing nut and adjust the table to align the top one-third of the board with the bit, then tighten the nut. Cut the tenon as you would on a standard table *(page 47)*, holding the workpiece flush against the feeding jig and the fence. **(Caution: Bit guard removed for clarity.)**

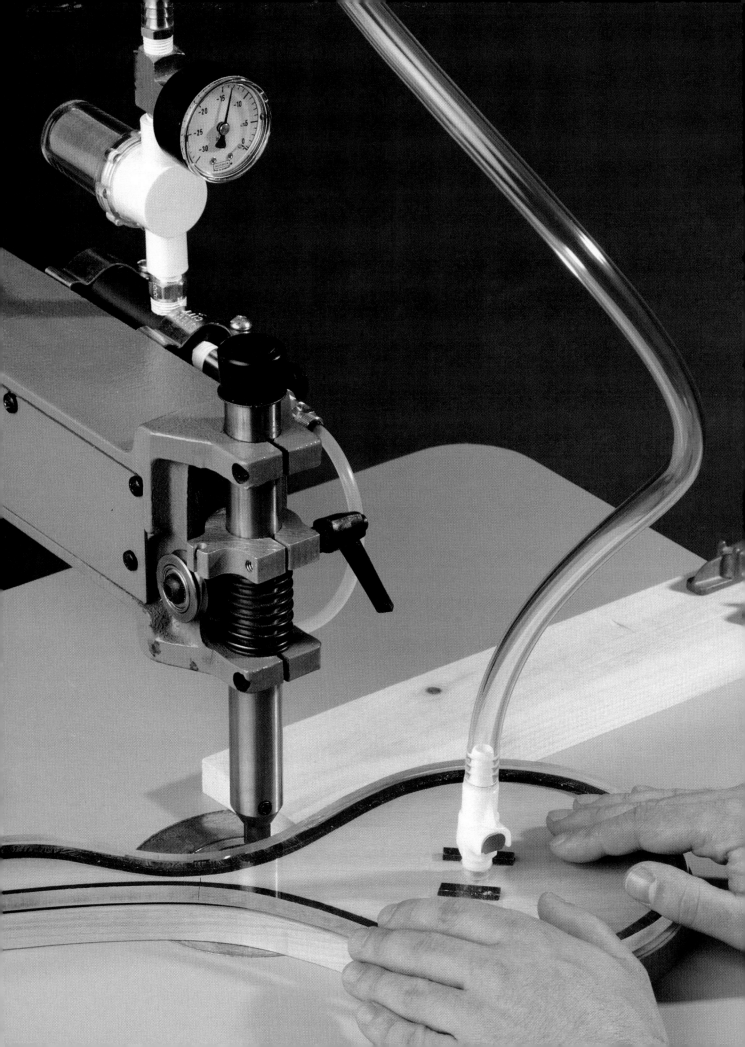

PATTERN ROUTING

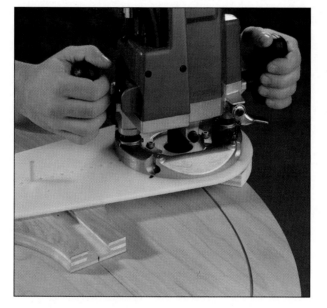

Paired with a commercial circle-cutting guide, an oval-cutting jig guides a router as it plows an elliptical groove for decorative inlay banding in a tabletop. The jig was used in a series of successively deeper passes to rout the table's outline. Refer to page 84 for instructions on making this easily adjustable jig.

Pattern routing is a precise and efficient method of creating multiple copies of a single contoured shape. The concept is easy to understand and the technique simple to execute: Once a template of the desired pattern is shaped and fastened to the workpiece, the router is guided by the cutout shape to replicate the design on the workpiece.

The two main ways of pattern routing are described starting on page 62. If you are using non-piloted bits, you need to fasten a template guide to your router's base plate and make your template slightly larger than the finished size. This compensates for the difference in diameters between the bit and the template guide. If you use piloted bits, on the other hand, a template guide is not used and the template can be exactly the same size as your finished piece.

Pattern routing has countless practical and decorative applications for woodworking, including the use of complementary templates. This method allows you to make templates with curved edges that are complementary images of each other, and then reproduce the patterns on two workpieces.

As shown on page 63, pattern routing can be done just as easily on a router table as with a hand-held router.

Another potentially complex task that is simplified by pattern routing is cutting recesses for inlays *(page 67)* and mortises for door hinges *(page 71)*. Using a template based on the size of the inlay or the hinge ensures that the recess will be precisely the right size.

If you are doing a lot of pattern routing you should consider buying a pin router. The inverted pin router shown on page 72 features a pin suspended over the table directly above the bit. The stock is guided along the pin, making the tool ideal for doing template work.

Although woodworkers have traditionally used fasteners to attach templates to workpieces in pattern routing—everything from double-sided tape and clamps to nails and screws—vacuum clamping offers several advantages over these methods. As shown on page 78, this clamping system is as strong as double-sided tape and easier to disengage, and unlike nails and screws, there is no risk of marring the workpiece or striking a metal fastener with the bit.

With its guide mechanism suspended above the work table, a pin router shapes the contours of a hand mirror. The stock is attached below a template of the desired pattern with a vacuum clamping system. The template rides against a guide pin over the table, while the bit, which is mounted directly below the pin, replicates the pattern on the workpiece.

ROUTING WITH TEMPLATES

The procedure you follow for pattern routing depends on the type of bit you are using. With a non-piloted bit, you must attach a template guide to the router base plate. A metal collar that surrounds the bit shank, the guide rides along the edge of the template, leaving the bit to shape the workpiece, which is clamped below the template. With a piloted bit *(page 63)*, a template guide is unnecessary, since the pilot bearing follows the pattern.

Pattern routing makes it possible to glue up a panel from boards with curved edges that mate together perfectly. As shown at left, all you need is a master template with the desired curve, a piloted straight bit with different-sized bearings, and a piloted flush-trimming bit. The bits are used to make the matching templates from the master and to shape the workpieces (page 64).

The template should be made from plywood or hardboard and cut to the desired pattern with a band saw or saber saw. To ensure there are no imperfections that the bit will transfer to the stock, carefully sand the edges of the template. As shown on page 63, you can also use ⅜-inch clear acrylic plastic as a template. Whichever material you choose, your pattern will be easier to produce if you are using piloted bits for routing. Since the cutter and pilot bearing are the same diameter, you can make the template the same size as the finished pieces you wish to produce. With a template guide, you must compensate for the difference between the cutter diameter and the diameter of the template collar.

BASIC PATTERN ROUTING

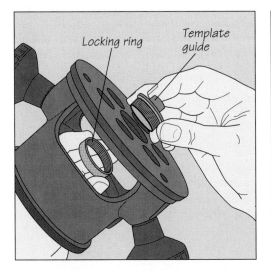

Using a template guide in a hand-held router

Remove the base plate from the router, insert the threaded part of the template guide through the opening in the middle of the sub-base *(above, left)*, and screw on the locking ring to hold the two together. Choose a template guide whose diameter is as close to that of the bit as possible without touching its cutting edges. Reinstall the base plate onto the router, then prepare a template that is slightly smaller than the finished piece to compensate for the difference between the bit diameter and the diameter of the template guide. Fasten the template atop the workpiece—in the example shown, double-sided tape was used—then clamp the assembly to a work surface. Holding the router with both hands, rest it on the template at one end with the bit clear of the stock and turn on the tool. Ease the bit into the workpiece, then feed the router toward the other end of the cut *(above, right)*, keeping the base flat on the template and the template guide flush against its edge.

Using a piloted bit

Fasten the template atop the workpiece and clamp the assembly to a work surface. With wood lips on each side of its curved corner, the template shown doubles as a corner-rounding jig. Make sure the top edges of the lips are flush with the top surface of the base and the lips are butted against the edges of your workpiece. Starting at one lip, cut the curve as you would with a template-guided bit *(page 62)*, feeding the cutter into the stock until the bit's pilot bearing contacts the template. Complete the cut to the other lip, making sure that the bearing is pressed against the edge of the pattern throughout the operation *(right)*.

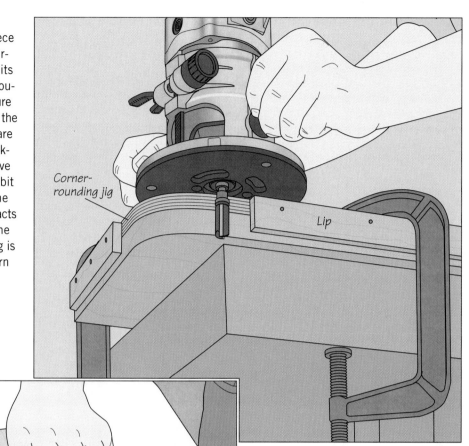

Pattern routing on a router table

To make it easier and safer to feed a template and workpiece across a router table, attach a board as a push block along the back edge of the template—in this case, the pattern is made from clear acrylic plastic. Fasten the stock to the template with double-sided tape and screw a pair of stop blocks to the template at either end of the workpiece to hold the stock securely. Next, cut a bit guard from a scrap board, sawing a notch from one edge to form a lip that will cover the cutter. Clamp the guard to the table. Turn on the router and slide the jig across the table to shape the workpiece *(left)*, keeping the template pressed against the bit's pilot bearing throughout the operation.

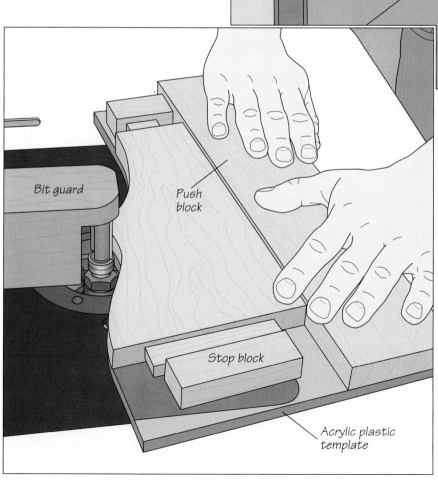

SHAPING MATCHING CURVED EDGES

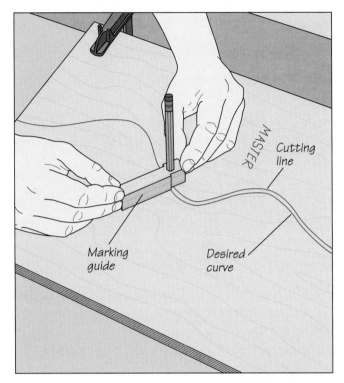

Marking guide

Cutting line

MASTER

Desired curve

1 Preparing the master template
In the operation presented on this and the following page, you can shape two curved edges that are matching images of each other. Start by forming a master template from which you will make the templates for the two pieces. Clamp the master to a work surface and mark the desired curve on it. Then, to compensate for the diameter of the pilot bearing you must use to guide the bit that cuts the right and left templates, mark a second line on the master template. This cutting line should be offset from the first one by one-half the difference between the bit diameter and the bearing diameter. In this case, the offset is $\frac{3}{16}$ inch to accommodate a $\frac{3}{8}$-inch bit and a $\frac{3}{4}$-inch bearing. To ensure that the cutting line is parallel to the original line, use a pencil in a shop-made marking guide. For the guide, drill a hole through a wood block near one end to fit a pencil snugly, then cut a notch on each edge $\frac{3}{16}$ inch from the center of the hole. As you mark the cutting line, align the notch shoulders with the original line and slide the guide from one end of the template to the other *(left)*. Cut the template along the second line on your band saw, then sand the cut edge smooth.

2 Making the right and left templates
Now use the master template to make the right and left templates from a single panel with one cut of the router. Set the panel on backup boards on a work surface, then clamp the master template on top, aligning the ends and edges of the template and panel. Next, install a $\frac{3}{8}$-inch up-spiral straight bit in your router and attach a $\frac{3}{4}$-inch-diameter pilot bearing to its shaft. Fasten a stop collar on each side of the bearing to secure it in place *(inset)*. Adjust the cutting depth so the bit will slice the template panel in two as you ride the bearing against the edge of the master template *(right)*. Keep the router flat on the master template throughout the cut.

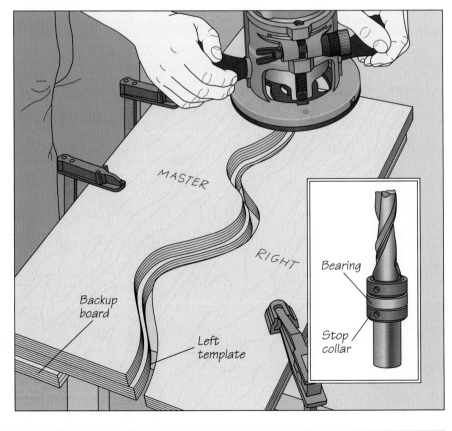

MASTER

RIGHT

Bearing

Stop collar

Backup board

Left template

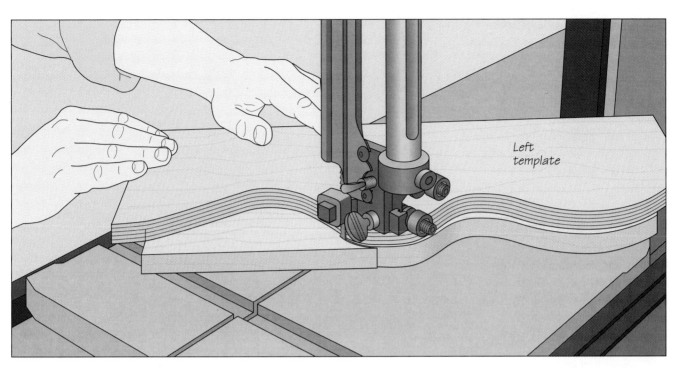

3 Rough-sizing the workpieces

Fasten each workpiece to its template, ensuring that the straight edges of the boards are aligned. Before trimming the pieces with the router, cut away the bulk of the waste on your band saw. With the edge of the template parallel to the blade, feed the left-hand workpiece into the cut, sawing to within about ⅛ inch of the template *(above)*. The remaining waste will be removed by the flush-trimming bit in step 4. Repeat the process to rough-size the right-hand workpiece, leaving about ½ inch of waste for the router to remove. The extra amount of waste will compensate for the larger bearing used in step 5.

4 Trimming the left-hand piece to final size

Install a top-piloted flush-cutting bit in the router and mount the tool in a router table. Clamp a shop-made guard over the bit *(page 63)*, then slide the left-hand template across the table to shape the left-hand workpiece *(right)*, keeping the template pressed against the bit's pilot bearing throughout the operation.

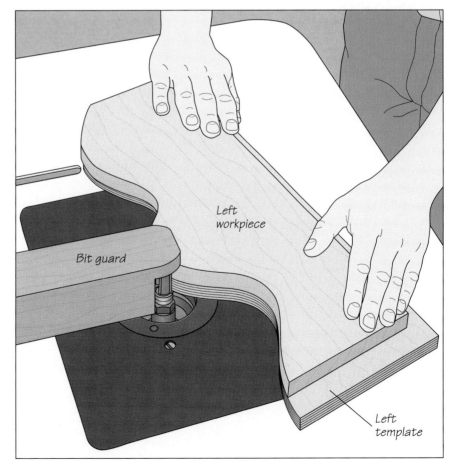

5 Shaping the right-hand workpiece

Remove the router from the table, reinstall the ⅜-inch up-spiral straight bit, and replace the ¾-inch pilot bearing with a 1⅛-inch one. The resulting offset (again, one half the difference between the bit diameter and the bearing diameter—or ⅜ inch) will compensate for the kerf removed by the cutter when it formed the left and right templates in step 2. This will ensure that the two workpieces match perfectly. Trim the workpiece the same way you shaped the left-hand one, keeping the template pressed against the bearing at all times *(right)*. Separate the work-pieces from their templates, then glue them together edge to edge, forming a panel like the one shown in the photo on page 62.

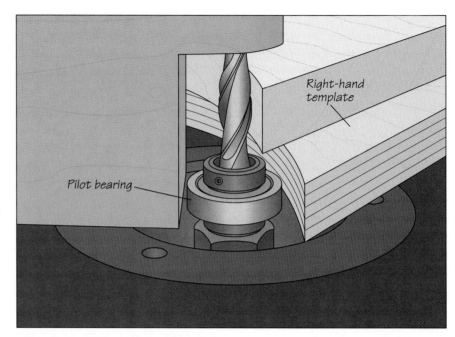

Right-hand template

Pilot bearing

PATTERN-ROUTING JIG

The jig shown at right is a time-saving device for shaping several copies of the same curved pattern. Make the template with one edge sawn to the desired profile, then cut your workpieces roughly to shape, oversizing the edge to be formed by about ⅛ inch. Position one workpiece on the template, aligning the cutting mark on the edge to be shaped with the curved edge of the template. Outline the workpiece on the tem-plate, then fasten three guide blocks to the template, lining up the edges of the blocks with the marked out-line. To complete the jig, screw a toggle clamp at each end of the long guide block.

Install a top-piloted flush-cutting bit in your router, mount the tool in a table, and set the cutting height so the pilot bearing will align with the

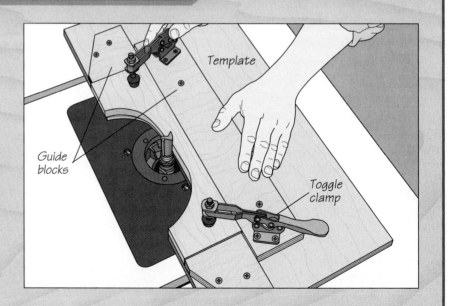

Template

Guide blocks

Toggle clamp

template. Secure the workpiece on the jig, making sure to butt the stock flush against the guide blocks. To make the cut, turn on the router with the jig clear of the bit. Holding the jig, feed the workpiece into the cut-ter. Apply slight pressure to press the template against the pilot bearing throughout the cut. **(Caution: Bit guard removed for clarity.)**

INLAY ROUTING

Fitted with a straight bit, a template guide, and a snap-on bushing, and guided by a shop-made template, a plunge router can plow a recess for an inlay quickly and accurately. The same setup can be used to trim the inlay to fit the recess perfectly. A wide range of inlays is available, from simple bands of exotic wood to elaborate marquetry patterns, as shown in the photo at right.

Routing the recess to the proper depth is one of the challenges of this operation. For marquetry inlay, the recess should be only slightly deeper than the inlay thickness—typically $\frac{1}{20}$ inch. If after gluing the inlay in place, it sits below the surrounding surface, you can sand the wood adjoining the inlay until the two surfaces are flush. To minimize tearout as you rout the recess or trim the inlay, use a downcut spiral bit.

A marquetry inlay, formed from a pattern of dyed wood set in a veneer, adorns a mahogany tabletop. The recess into which the inlay is set was cut with a template-guided router.

GLUING MARQUETRY INLAY IN PLACE

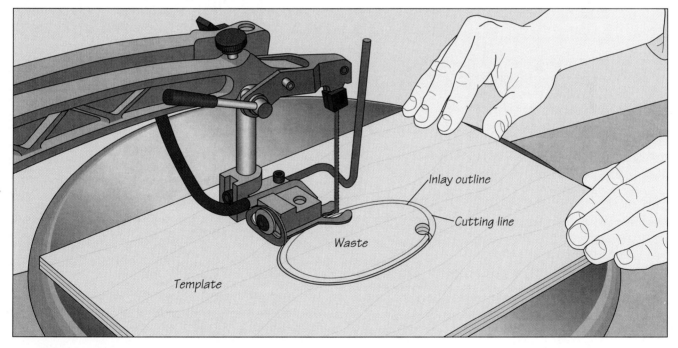

Inlay outline

Cutting line

Waste

Template

1 Making the template
The key to trimming an inlay and routing a perfectly matching recess for it is to use the same template for both operations. Outline the inlay on a piece of plywood, then draw a second outline ¼ inch larger than the first to allow for the width of the bit

and template guide. Drill a hole to fit a scroll saw blade through the waste portion of the template. Feed the blade through the hole, fasten it to the saw, and cut just to the waste side of your second outline *(above)*. Sand up to the marked line.

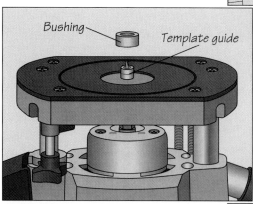

Bushing

Template guide

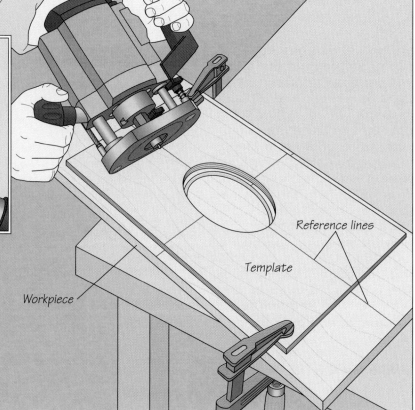

Reference lines

Template

Workpiece

2 Routing the recess

For best results, rout the recess and trim the inlay with a commercial inlay-routing set, which consists of a bit, a template guide, and a bushing that snaps onto the guide. You rout the recess with the entire assembly on your router's base plate *(inset)*, but remove the bushing for trimming the inlay *(step 3)*. This will compensate for the bit and template guide diameter, and ensure a seamless fit. For the recess, mark references lines on both the template and the workpiece that intersect at the center of their top faces. Then set the workpiece on a table, position the template on top so the reference marks all align, and clamp the assembly in place. Set the router flat on the template with the bushing butted against the inside edge of the template. Plunge the bit into the stock, then feed the tool in a clockwise direction. Complete the cut *(above, right)*, keeping the bushing in contact with the edge of the template throughout the operation.

SHOP TIP

An oversized sub-base for large recesses
It can be difficult to rout an inlay recess and keep the router flat when the recess is larger than the tool's standard sub-base. To remedy the problem, make a substitute sub-base from a piece of ⅜-inch clear acrylic cut wider than the recess outline. Remove the standard sub-base and use it as a template to drill the mounting and bit clearance holes in the acrylic base. Then fasten the new sub-base to the router and cut the recess as described above.

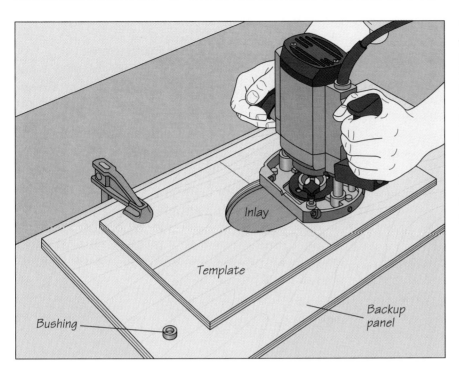

3 Trimming the inlay

Set a backup panel on a work surface and fix the inlay to it using double-sided tape, making sure to attach the tape to the backing-paper side of the inlay. Position the template on top, centering its opening over the inlay, then clamp the assembly to the table. Remove the bushing from the router bit, but leave the template guide in place, and trim the inlay the same way you cut the recess, keeping the guide pressed against the inside edge of the template throughout *(left)*.

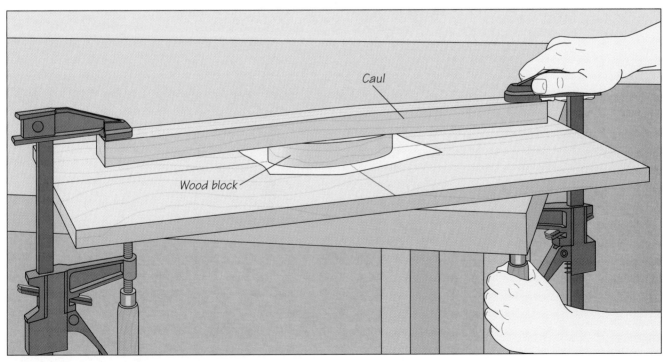

4 Gluing the inlay in place

Carefully remove the double-sided tape and backing paper from the inlay, then test-fit it in the recess. If the inlay is still slightly oversized, place it a microwave oven set to high heat for 10 to 30 seconds to shrink it. Once you are satisfied with the fit, spread a thin coating of glue in the recess and set the inlay in place. Cover the inlay with a piece of wax paper then top it with a wood block slightly smaller than the inlay. Clamp a caul across the block to secure it *(above)*. When the glue has cured, remove the block and sand the inlay or the surrounding wood to make the surfaces flush.

GLUING IN INLAY BORDER BANDING

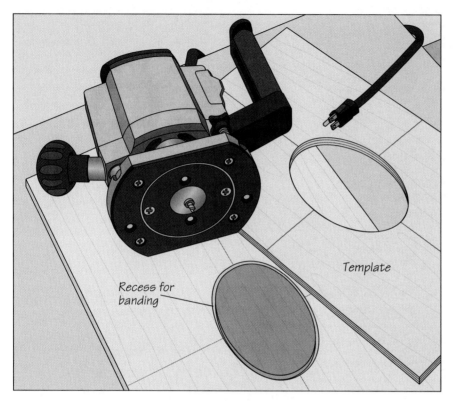

Recess for banding

Template

1 Routing the border recess
With the same template used to rout an inlay recess and trim the inlay *(page 67)*, you can plow a narrow recess around the inlay for a strip of banding. Once the adhesive securing the inlay has cured, clamp the template to the workpiece so its opening is centered over the inlay. Set the router's cutter depth ⅛ inch deeper than the thickness of the template, then rout the recess the same way you trimmed the inlay *(page 69)*, making sure the template guide is pressed against the template throughout the cut. Unclamp the template *(left)*.

2 Installing the banding
Make the banding from a wood species that contrasts with the panel and the inlay. Cut the strip about 2 inches longer than the perimeter of the recess, beveling one end; since you will be installing the banding on edge, make it slightly wider than the recess depth and its thickness equal to the recess width. If the banding is stiff and difficult to bend around the recess, soak it first in hot water for 30 minutes. Spread some glue in the recess, insert the beveled end, and pack the banding around the recess *(right)*, bending the strip and tapping it in place with a wooden mallet as you go. Mark a cutting line across the banding at the point where the ends meet. Then, with a backup board to protect the workpiece, cut a matching bevel at the straight end and finish inserting the banding in the recess. Sand the banding flush with the surrounding wood.

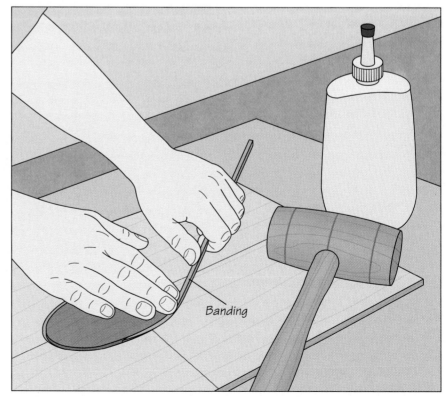

Banding

ROUTING HINGE MORTISES

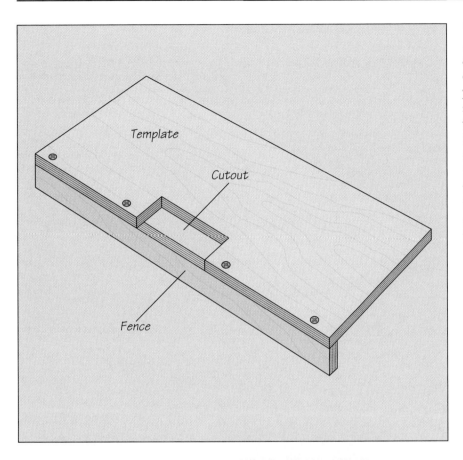

1 Building the jig
A jig like the one shown at left will allow your router to cut hinge mortises quickly and accurately. To make the cuts, you will need to equip your router with a straight bit and a template guide. Build the template from a piece of ¾-inch plywood. Size it wide enough to support the router. Outline the hinge leaf on the template; increase the dimensions to compensate for the template guide and the thickness of the fence, which is also made from ¾-inch plywood. Cut out the template, then attach the fence with countersunk screws.

2 Routing the mortise
Secure the workpiece edge-up in a vise. Mark the hinge outline on the stock and clamp the template in position, aligning the cutout with the outline on the edge and butting the fence against the inside face of the workpiece. Make the cut *(bottom)* by moving the router in small clockwise circles, then remove the jig and, if necessary, square the corners with a chisel.

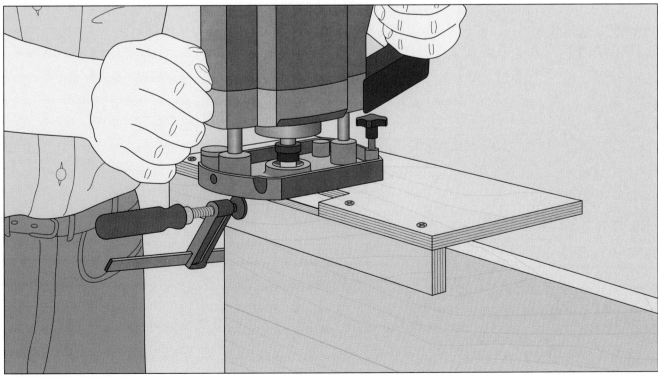

PIN ROUTER

Like a table-mounted router, the pin router allows you to feed a workpiece across a table while a cutter below the surface shapes or grooves the stock. But unlike router tables, pin routers feature a metal pin that follows a pattern while the bit aligned below it replicates the design on the workpiece. Standard pin routers suspend the cutting assembly above the table and have the guide pin mounted in the tabletop. In the "inverted" pin router shown at right, the router assembly hangs below the table and the guide pin is aligned above it—a much safer arrangement, since the bit is usually covered by the workpiece.

The pin router can be used exactly like a router table, if necessary. Simply raise the guide pin as high as it will go and shape your workpiece using a piloted bit or a non-piloted bit and a fence.

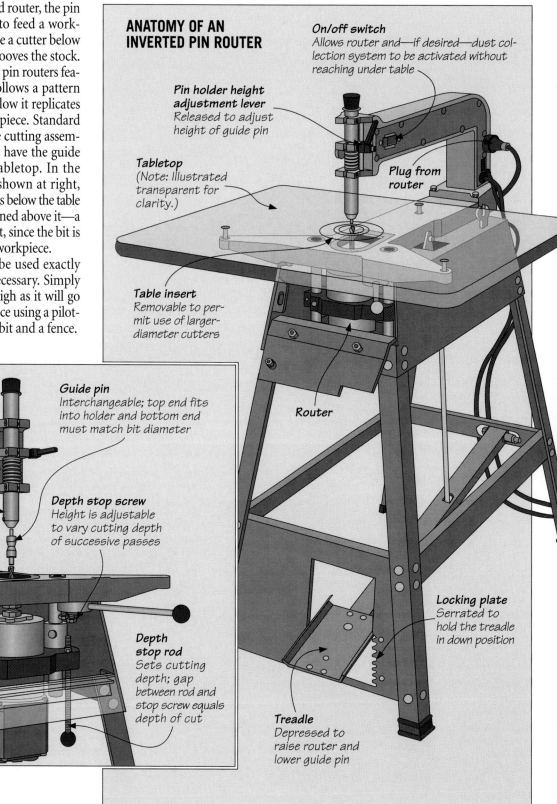

ANATOMY OF AN INVERTED PIN ROUTER

On/off switch
Allows router and—if desired—dust collection system to be activated without reaching under table

Pin holder height adjustment lever
Released to adjust height of guide pin

Plug from router

Tabletop
(Note: Illustrated transparent for clarity.)

Table insert
Removable to permit use of larger-diameter cutters

Router

Pin holder
Secures guide pin

Guide pin
Interchangeable; top end fits into holder and bottom end must match bit diameter

Depth stop screw
Height is adjustable to vary cutting depth of successive passes

Depth stop rod
Sets cutting depth; gap between rod and stop screw equals depth of cut

Locking plate
Serrated to hold the treadle in down position

Treadle
Depressed to raise router and lower guide pin

AN OVERARM PIN ROUTING ATTACHMENT

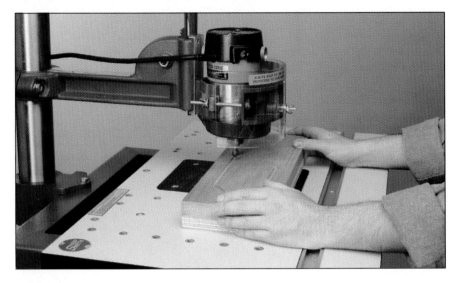

Suspended in a conventional pin routing attachment, a router plows a groove on a panel. A template with the desired pattern is attached to the underside of the workpiece and a guide pin located in the table directly below the bit ensures that the pattern is accurately reproduced.

MAKING A HAND MIRROR ON A PIN ROUTER

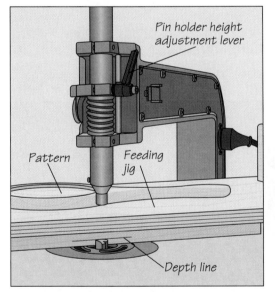

Pin holder height adjustment lever

Pattern

Feeding jig

Depth line

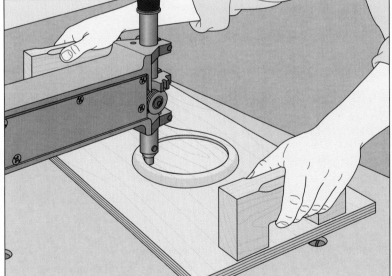

1 Cutting the recess for the mirror
Use double-sided tape to fasten a mirror blank to one side of a plywood feeding jig. Attaching a handle at each end of the jig will make it easier to maneuver. Fasten the pattern—in this case, a prototype mirror—to the opposite side of the jig, making sure the outline of the pattern is fully contained within the edges of the blank on the other side. Mark the depth of the recess on an edge of the blank and set the assembly on the pin router table. Depress the treadle, release the pin holder height adjustment lever, and slide the holder down until it fits within the recess in the mirror without contacting the surface. Tighten

the lever. Depress the treadle further to align the bit with the depth line *(above, left)*, then turn the depth-stop rod until it contacts the stop screw above it. Release the treadle. Next, center the recess in the mirror under the guide pin, turn on the router, and depress the treadle fully, plunging the bit into the workpiece. Holding the handles of the jig, feed the workpiece in a circular pattern, keeping the guide pin flush against the edges of the mirror recess *(above, right)*. This will cut a groove around the rim of the recess in the workpiece. Remove the remaining waste with a series of circular cuts.

2 Routing the profile

With the router turned off, adjust the height of the guide pin so the gap between its tip and the base of the jig is about ¹⁄₁₆ inch. Next, adjust the height of the bit to cut slightly deeper than the thickness of the workpiece. Then rout the profile of the mirror the same way you plowed the recess, pressing the guide pin against the contours of the pattern throughout *(right)*. To avoid burning the wood, be sure to keep the jig moving until the end of the cut. In addition, if the profile is too thick to cut in a single pass, you can make several shallow passes by adjusting the stop screws to different cutting heights and switching stop screws after each pass.

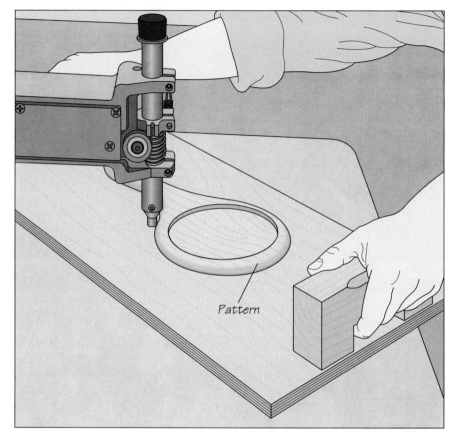

Pattern

3 Separating the workpiece from the jig

Once you have cut the profile of the mirror, turn the jig over *(below)* and pry the mirror and the waste wood from the underside of the jig base.

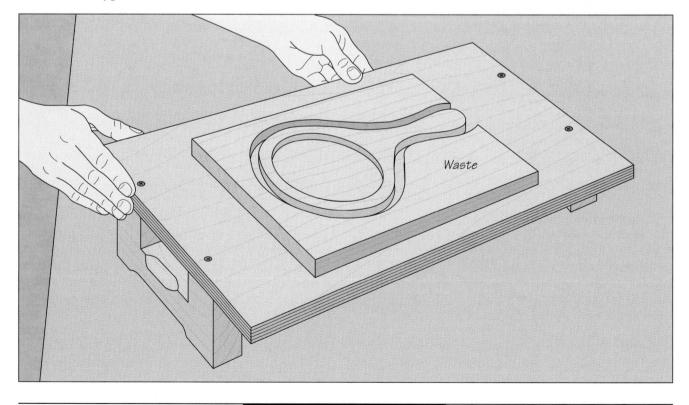

Waste

EDGE FORMING WITH THE PIN ROUTER

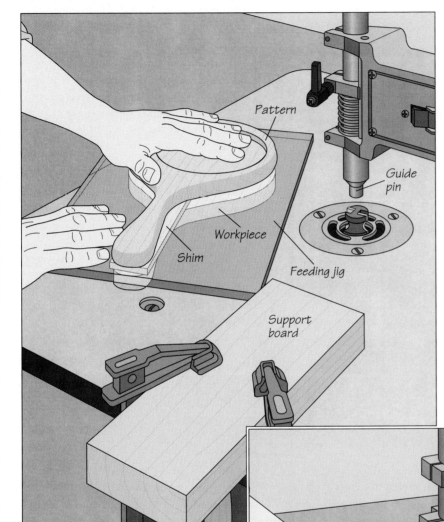

Pattern

Guide pin

Workpiece

Shim

Feeding jig

Support board

1 Setting up the cut
Install an edge-forming bit in the pin router—in this example, a bull nose bit is shown—and adjust its height to shape the edge of your blank. Cut the workpiece roughly to size on the band saw, then fix it with double-sided tape to a ⅜-inch-thick acrylic-plastic feeding jig that is slightly larger than the blank; place a shim between the blank and the jig so the bit will not cut into the acrylic. The jig will protect your hands from the bit and, being clear plastic, will allow you to view the cutting action. Next, fix your pattern to the opposite side of the jig, making sure to align it exactly over the blank, and adjust the guide pin to ride along the pattern as you make the cut. Clamp a support board to the table in line with the cutter and turn on the router. Holding the jig and pattern flat on the table, butt the back corner of the jig against the support board *(left)*, then pivot the jig and blank into the bit until the guide pin contacts the pattern and the cutter bites into the workpiece.

2 Molding the edge
Keeping a firm hold of the jig and pattern, feed the workpiece along the table against the direction of bit rotation *(right)*. Make certain to press the pattern against the template until you return to your starting point. Once you complete the cut, pry the workpiece from the jig.

STRAIGHT ROUTING ON A PIN ROUTER

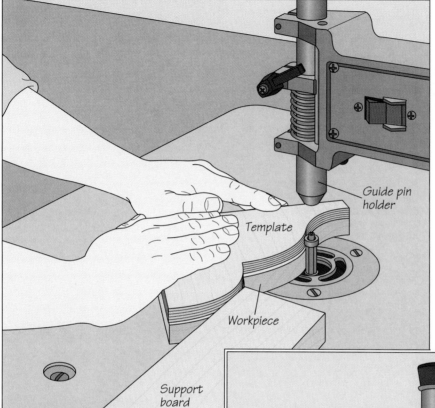

Guide pin holder

Template

Workpiece

Support board

Pattern routing

As the illustrations on this page show, you can use an inverted pin router for edge-shaping as you would a router table. Start by removing the guide pin from its holder and raising the holder to its highest setting. For pattern routing with a piloted bit, fasten the workpiece to your template and adjust the bit's cutting height so the pilot bearing will ride against the template with the blank flat on the table. Clamp a support board to the table in line with the bit and turn on the router. Holding the template and blank with both hands, press one edge of the assembly flush against the support board. Then pivot the workpiece into the cutter and slowly feed it against the direction of bit rotation *(left)*. Keep the template pressed against the pilot bearing throughout the cut.

Shaping a straight board

With the help of a shop-built fence, you can mold the edges of straight stock on a pin router. Make a fence as you would for a router table *(page 44)*, then clamp it to the pin router table, aligning its front face with the bit's pilot bearing. To support the stock, use three featherboards, clamping one to the table and two to the fence, one on each side of the cutter. (Note: In the illustration, the featherboard on the out-feed side of the fence has been removed for clarity.) Feed the workpiece across the table, pressing the edge flush against the fence and the face flat on the table *(right)*. Finish the pass with a push stick.

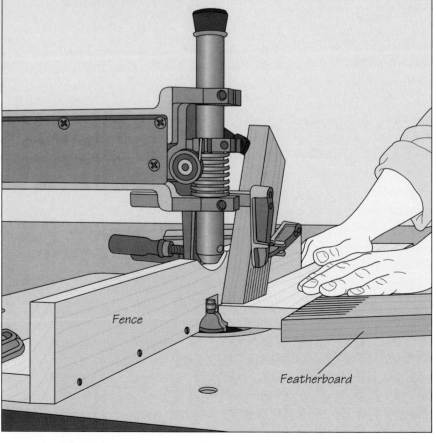

Fence

Featherboard

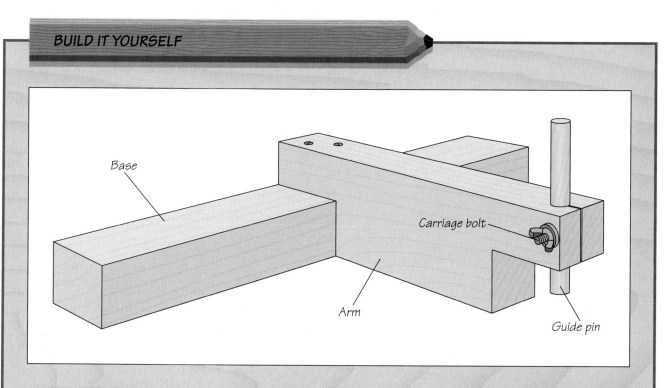

BUILD IT YOURSELF

Base

Carriage bolt

Arm

Guide pin

SHOP-BUILT PIN ROUTER

Although you cannot plunge the bit into a workpiece from below, you can perform the other pin routing procedures shown on pages 73 to 75 using a router table and the shop-built jig shown here. As in an inverted pin router, the bit is situated below the table and an adjustable guide pin is located above.

Cut the base of the jig from hardwood; make it as long as your router table. The T-shaped arm, also made of hardwood, should be long enough to extend over the bit when the jig base is clamped to the edge of the router table. For the guide pin, bore a ½-inch-diameter hole through the top of the arm and cut a 5-inch-length of dowel. Then saw a kerf into the tip that intersects with the hole and drill another hole through the side of the arm for a ¼-inch carriage bolt. Screw the arm to the base and use a bolt, washer and wing nut to clamp the guide pin in the arm.

To use the jig, install a ½-inch straight bit in the router and mount the tool in the table. Clamp the jig to the table so the guide pin is directly above the bit. Loosen the wing nut, adjust the guide pin so that it sits slightly above the bit and tighten the nut. Shape an edge as you would on a pin router (page 76). Be sure you keep the template butted against the pin throughout the operation.

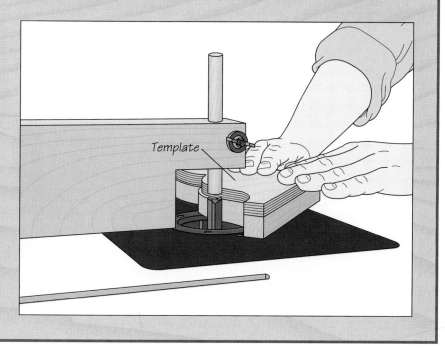

Template

VACUUM CLAMPING

Vacuum clamping is a reliable and simple way to fasten templates and workpieces together. The systems shown in this section of the chapter offer as much holding power as mechanical clamps and greater convenience without risk of damage to the stock. The only requirement is that mating surfaces be flat and smooth.

There are two common vacuum-clamping systems. The venturi system *(below)* is relatively inexpensive to set up, but you will need a compressor with ½-horsepower capable of delivering 60 to 80 PSI. The system shown on page 82 relies on a vacuum pump rated at 3 cubic feet per minute or higher. In either case, vacuum tape is fastened to both sides of a commercially available bench plate, which is capable of clamping on two sides. The plate is then sandwiched between the workpiece and template. The tubing from the venturi or pump is attached to the outlets on the bench plate—one for the workpiece side and one for the template side. The venturi or pump then sucks air from cavities on both sides.

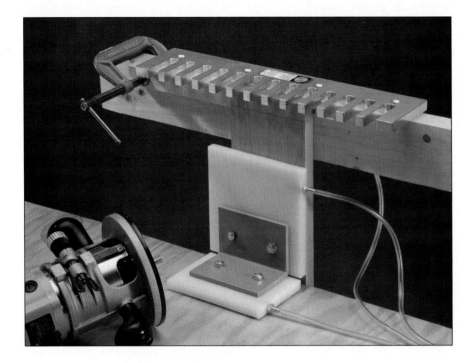

The setup shown at left relies on three vacuum tubes to hold a drawer side against a commercial dovetail jig. Two of the tubes are connected to an L-shaped vacuum-clamping jig; the vertical section holds the workpiece in position and the base secures the entire assembly to the bench. The vacuum tube connected to the dovetail jig's backing board fastens the jig to the workpiece.

ESSENTIAL PARTS OF A VACUUM-CLAMPING SYSTEM

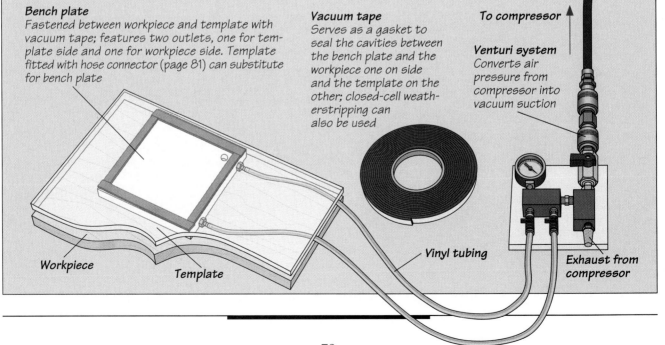

Bench plate
Fastened between workpiece and template with vacuum tape; features two outlets, one for template side and one for workpiece side. Template fitted with hose connector (page 81) can substitute for bench plate

Vacuum tape
Serves as a gasket to seal the cavities between the bench plate and the workpiece one on side and the template on the other; closed-cell weatherstripping can also be used

To compressor

Venturi system
Converts air pressure from compressor into vacuum suction

Vinyl tubing

Exhaust from compressor

Workpiece

Template

VACUUM-ROUTING WITH A BENCH PLATE

Bench plate

1 Preparing the bench plate
Apply four strips of closed-cell vacuum tape to each side of the bench plate, forming a rectangle with no gaps *(above)*. Next, screw the fittings at the ends of the tubes from the vacuum source to the outlets on the bench plate.

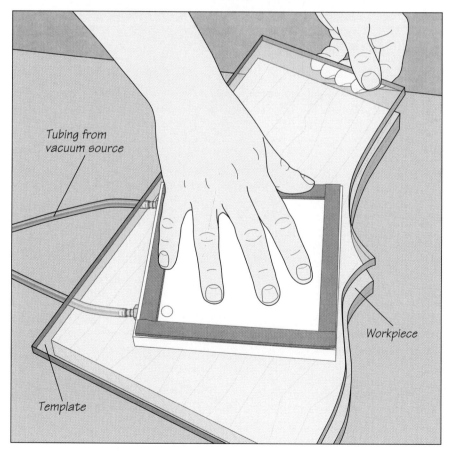

Tubing from vacuum source

Workpiece

Template

2 Anchoring the workpiece and template to the bench plate
Cut the workpiece roughly to size, then set it on a work surface. Position the bench plate on the stock, making sure the tape strips are flat on the workpiece. Turn on the vacuum source to the workpiece-side of the bench plate and press the plate on the workpiece to seal the vacuum. Air pressure will hold the two together. Next, position the template on the bench plate *(left)*, aligning the straight edges of the template and the workpiece. Turn on the vacuum to the template-side of the bench plate and press down to attach the pattern to the plate.

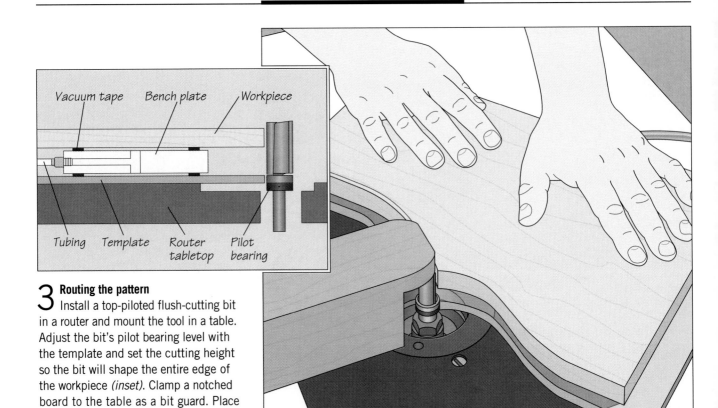

Vacuum tape   Bench plate   Workpiece

Tubing   Template   Router   Pilot
tabletop   bearing

3 Routing the pattern

Install a top-piloted flush-cutting bit in a router and mount the tool in a table. Adjust the bit's pilot bearing level with the template and set the cutting height so the bit will shape the entire edge of the workpiece *(inset)*. Clamp a notched board to the table as a bit guard. Place the bench-plate assembly template-side down on the table, turn on the router, and ease the stock into the bit until the template contacts the pilot bearing *(above, right)*. Complete the cut, moving against the direction of bit rotation and keeping the template flat on the router table and the edge of the template pressed flush against the bearing.

SHOP TIP

Customizing a bench plate for a small workpiece
A workpiece that is smaller than a bench plate cannot normally be vacuum-clamped to the plate. However, you can temporarily reduce the surface area of the bench plate that will be under vacuum pressure by applying an additional strip of tape, creating a rectangle slightly smaller than the workpiece. Then anchor the workpiece to the plate as described on page 79. Remember to remove the extra strip of tape to shape a workpiece that is larger than the bench plate.

A SHOP-MADE BENCH PLATE

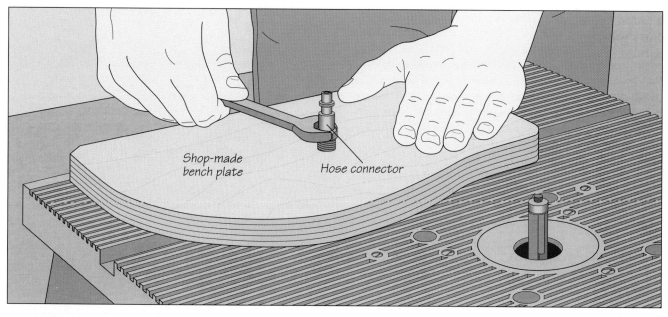

1 Preparing a template for vacuum routing

For patterns you rout frequently, you can convert a plywood template into a shop-made bench plate, rather than using a commercial one. Bore an outlet hole through the middle of the template for a vacuum pump's threaded hose connector and apply vacuum tape along the perimeter of its underside; make sure there are no gaps between adjacent pieces of tape. Then use a wrench to attach the hose connector to the top of the plate in the outlet hole (above).

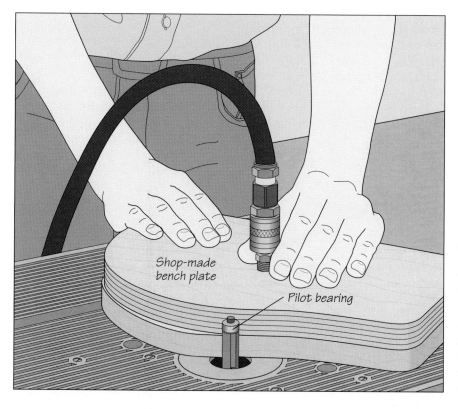

2 Shaping the workpiece

Place the bench plate tape-side down centered on top of the workpiece. Attach the tubing from the vacuum source to the hose connector and switch on the compressor or vacuum pump. Then install a bottom-piloted bit in the router and shape the pattern as you would with a commercial bench-plate setup (page 80), except in this case the workpiece is flat on the table while the plate faces up (left).

A VACUUM PUMP SYSTEM

The vacuum clamping system illustrated at right is similar to the venturi method presented on page 78, except that it relies on a pump as a vacuum source. The model shown is a ⅓-horsepower oilless pump, which draws air at a maximum of 4.5 cubic feet per minute. The hose features a quick coupler that attaches to a commercial bench plate or to a connector that is screwed into a hole through the template. The vacuum tape seals the cavity between the template and workpiece, or between the bench plate and the workpiece and template.

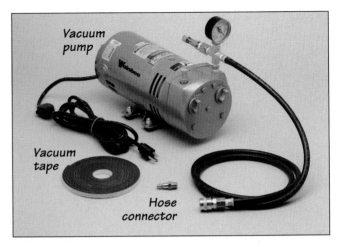

Vacuum pump

Vacuum tape

Hose connector

BUILD IT YOURSELF

A VACUUM TABLE

As an alternative to clamping a workpiece to a bench, the vacuum table shown below can secure a workpiece for edge shaping with a hand-held router. With no clamps to get in the way of the router, this system offers more convenience than conventional clamping.

For the top, cut a piece of plastic laminate and glue it down to a base of ¾-inch plywood as you would for a shop-built router table *(page 40).*

You can make the pieces any suitable size, but cutting them 8 inches wide by 16 inches long will produce 1,280 pounds of clamping force. Drill a hole through the top near one edge and midway between the ends; size the hole for a threaded hose connector and fasten the connector to the top from underneath. Screw a solid-wood 1-by-2 spacer as long as the top is wide to the top's underside along each end; the outside edges of the spacers should be flush with the ends of the top.

Table-top

Hose connector

Spacer

Next, apply four strips of vacuum tape around the perimeter of the top, forming a rectangular cavity; make sure that there are no gaps between the strips.

To use the vacuum table, secure it to your workbench and center the workpiece on the table, ensuring that the tape strips make solid contact with the stock. Turn on your vacuum source, then use a router fitted with a bottom-piloted bit to shape the edges of the workpiece, making sure to keep the pilot bearing pressed against the edge of the stock throughout the operation *(above).*

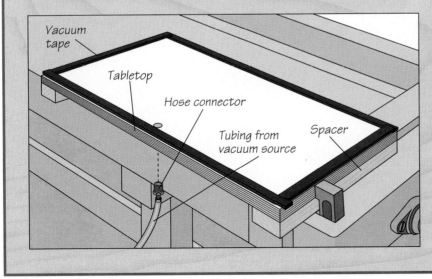

Vacuum tape

Tabletop

Hose connector

Tubing from vacuum source

Spacer

ADJUSTABLE ROUTING GUIDE

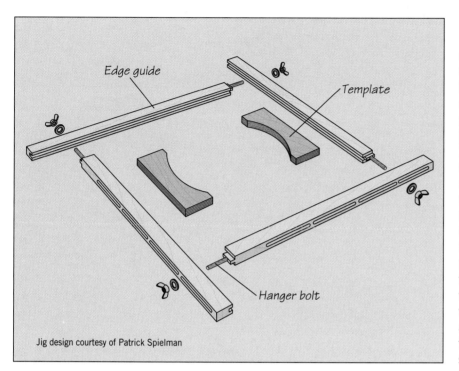

Edge guide

Template

Hanger bolt

Jig design courtesy of Patrick Spielman

1 Building the jig
The jig shown at left is ideal for routing rectangular grooves; it can also be fitted with templates for curved cuts. Rather than following the pattern with a piloted bit or a non-piloted bit and a template guide, you feed the router base plate along the jig's inside edges. Saw the guides from 1-by-2 stock and rout a groove ⅜ inch deep and wide along the inside edge of each one. Cut a two-shouldered tenon at one end of each guide to fit in the grooves and bore a pilot hole into the middle of each tenon for a ⅜-inch-diameter hanger bolt. Screw the bolts in place, leaving the machine thread protruding to feed through the adjacent edge guide and lock with a washer and wing nut. Finally, rout ⅜-inch-wide mortises through the guides; start about 3½ inches from the end with the tenon and make the mortises 4 inches long, separating them with about ½ inch of wood. Assemble the jig by slipping the tenons and bolts through the grooves and mortises of the adjacent guide and installing the washers and nuts. For curves, make templates like those shown in the illustration.

2 Routing the groove
Outline the pattern on your stock and lay it on a work surface. Loosen the wing nuts of the jig and position it on the stock so the edge guides frame the outline. Place the router flat on the workpiece and align the bit with one edge of the outline. Butt one of the edge guides flush against the router base plate. Repeat on the other edges until all guides and templates are in position. (Use double-sided tape to secure the templates to the workpiece.) Tighten the wing nuts and clamp the jig and workpiece to the table. After plunging the bit into the stock, make the cut in a clockwise direction, keeping the base plate flush against the edge guide or template at all times. For repeat cuts, simply clamp the jig to the new workpiece and rout the pattern *(left)*.

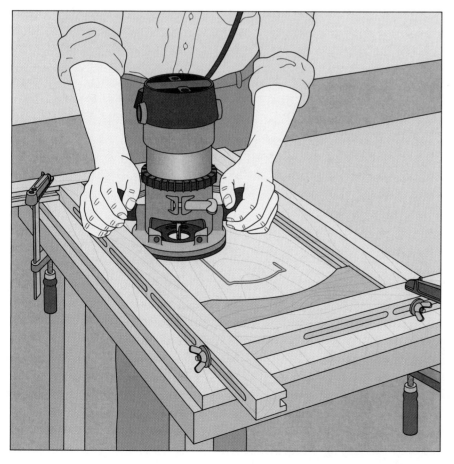

BUILD IT YOURSELF

OVAL-CUTTING JIG

Paired with a router and a circle-cutting guide, the jig shown at right enables you to rout ovals of any shape and size. Rather than fixing the guide to a single point, as you would to cut a circle, the jig anchors the guide to two sliding dowels. The slides are positioned so the distance between the bit and the dowels determines the long and short axes of the oval. As the router is rotated around the jig, the tool moves in an elliptical pattern, cutting a perfect oval.

Make the jig base from a piece of 15-inch-square ¾-inch plywood. To cut the channels in the base, install a dovetail bit in a router, mount the tool in a table, and set the cutting height to ⁷⁄₁₆ inch. Align the middle of one end of the base with the bit and butt the fence against the adjoining edge. Clamp a featherboard to the table flush

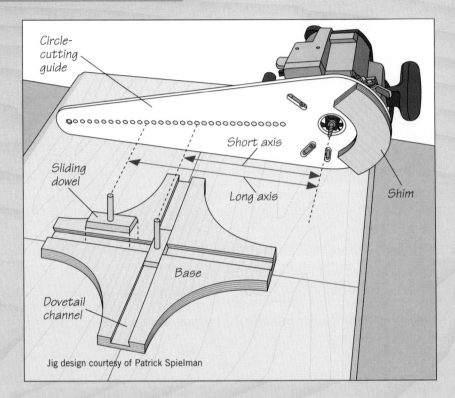

Circle-cutting guide

Short axis

Long axis

Sliding dowel

Base

Dovetail channel

Shim

Jig design courtesy of Patrick Spielman

against the the opposite edge. Then feed the base across the table, routing a dovetail channel. Rotate the piece 90° and repeat, cutting a second channel perpendicular to the first one. Shift the fence ⅛ inch away from the bit, reposition the featherboard accordingly, and make four more passes, running each edge of the base along the fence. Continue until the channel is about 1 inch wide *(left)*. To finish preparing the base, use your band saw to cut an arc out of each corner; this will prevent the router from striking the base when you use the jig.

Cut the sliding dowels on your table saw, making both slides from a single board at least 12 inches long. Measure the edges of the dovetail channel with a sliding bevel and transfer the angle to the saw blade. Then rip a bevel along both edges of the slide stock, guiding the board along the rip fence and feeding it with a push stick *(right)*. Size the board to slide smoothly in the dovetail channel. Crosscut two 2-inch-long slides from the board, then drill a hole for a ¼-inch dowel into the center of each slide. Finally, cut two 1¼-inch-long dowels and glue them into the slides.

To prepare the circle-cutting guide, drill a row of ¼-inch-diameter holes along its centerline, spacing them at ½-inch intervals. To ensure that the router sits level when it rotates around the jig, cut an arc-shaped shim the same thickness as the jig base, sized to fit on the underside of the guide between the bit clearance hole and the

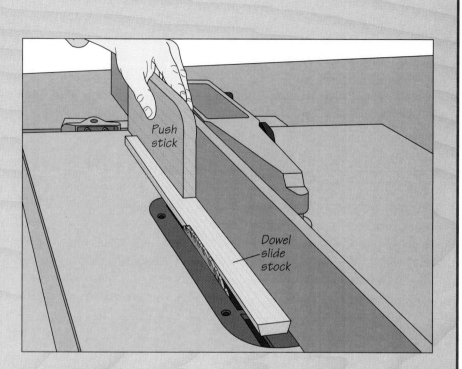

Push stick

Dowel slide stock

wide end of the guide. Fasten the guide and the shim to the router base plate.

To use the jig, clamp your workpiece to a table and mark perpendicular reference lines from edge to edge and end to end, intersecting at the center of the surface. Then position the base on the workpiece, aligning the center of the dovetail channels with the reference lines. Mark the long and short axes of the oval you want to rout on the underside of the guide, measuring from the bit to the appropriate holes. Spread a little wax in the dovetail channels and slip one sliding dowel into each channel. Place the guide over the base, fitting the dowels into the marked holes. With the shim flat on the workpiece and the guide flush against the jig base, plunge the bit into the stock and feed the router around the base to cut the oval *(left)*.

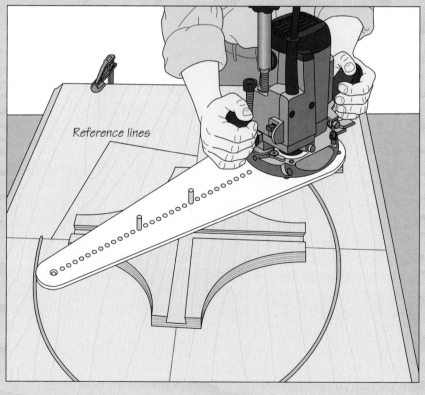

Reference lines

JOINERY

The router is by far the most adaptable joint-making tool in the workshop. Numbers of commercial jigs and router bits have been developed over the years that enable the tool to produce many common joints, such as dovetails, box joints, and mortise-and-tenons, and perform other, not so common, operations. The jig shown in the photo at right, for example, relies on router-like cutting action to cut pocket holes. Although the jig can accomplish little else, it does the job of assembling face frames quickly and precisely. Other commercial router jigs are illustrated starting on page 88. Some of these devices are expensive, and if you plan only to make the occasional joint, you may be better off doing the work with hand tools. But if your upcoming projects include a lot of repetitive work—a chest of drawers with plenty of dovetailed joints or a series of doors with mortise and tenons, for example—these jigs can quickly prove to be a worthwhile investment.

Although the router is seldom used freehand to cut joints, very few router joinery techniques absolutely require an expensive commercial jig. The only accessory needed to rout several common joints is a router table. With a three-wing slotting cutter and an auxiliary fence on your table, for example, you can produce double dado joints *(page 90)* for assembling drawers. Another interlocking joint that is simple to cut on the router table is the lock miter joint *(page 96)*. A table will also enable you to convert your router into a plate joiner; the simple setup shown on page 94 simplifies cutting slots for the biscuits, which swell when glue is applied, creating a sturdy, invisible joint. And although through dovetails are traditionally crafted by hand or routed with the aid of a commercial jig, the technique beginning on page 104 shows how to create this strong, attractive joint on the router table aided only by a miter gauge.

You can enhance your router's joint-cutting capacity with a variety of shop-built jigs. The simple T-shaped jig shown on page 92, for example, is ideal for routing half-lap joints. The biscuit-slot jig *(page 95)* transforms a hand-held router into a plate joiner. And the jig shown on page 97—essentially a work surface with a slot cut through it—will serve as well as a commercial device for routing mortises.

With its router-like cutter, the commercial jig shown above cuts precise pocket holes quickly. With a face-frame rail clamped in the jig, the bit is pivoted into the face of the board to cut the pocket hole. The rail will be screwed to a stile. Refer to page 102 for instructions on building a shop-made version of the jig.

The laminate trimmer shown at left routs out the waste between the pins of a half-blind dovetail joint. With its offset base, the trimmer allows a user to focus all downward pressure on the work surface, which helps prevent the tool from wobbling. The base rides along an edge guide, ensuring that the depth of the sockets remains uniform across the board.

COMMERCIAL JIGS

There are scores of commercial router jigs available today. Some, like the Keller jig *(page 89)*, are as simple as a set of metal templates that guide the router as it cuts a joint. Others, like the WoodRat shown below, are elaborate, adjustable devices that can be set up to cut several joints. The four jigs shown on this and the following page represent a cross section of what is available in terms of versatility and price. The advantage of a jig is that it permits you to produce a lot of joints precisely and quickly. And, it often eliminates the need for hand-work skills. It is much harder, for example, to cut a good-fitting dovetail with a hand saw and chisel than it is to use a router and a jig. But there is a tradeoff: Many seasoned woodworkers complain that nothing can match the look of a handcrafted joint. The regular spacing of the dovetails of a fixed template is too predictable and looks too machine-made, they say. The Leigh jig solves that problem by offering a way to adjust the spacing and width of the pins and tails. But of course, that extra flexibility comes

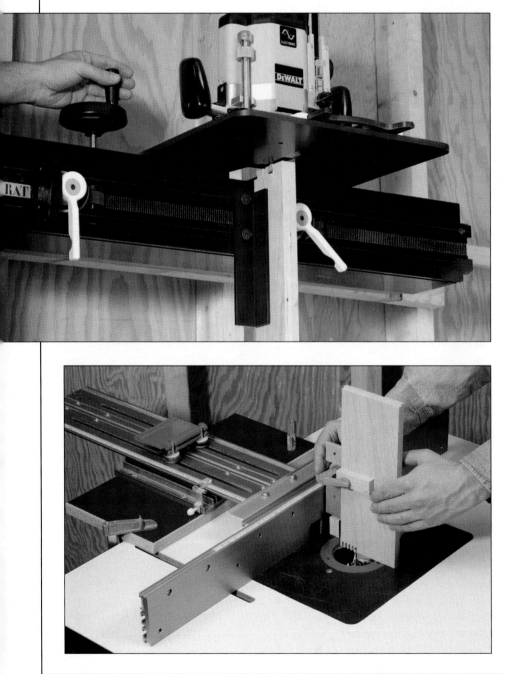

WoodRat

This is a sophisticated jig capable of cutting a wide range of joints, including through and half-blind dovetails, lap joints, mortise-and-tenons, tongue-and-grooves, and rabbets. The router is held upright on a metal plate on the jig and one or more workpieces are clamped on a sliding bar below the plate. The router can be guided along the plate into a stationary workpiece, or the stock can be fed into the bit by turning a handwheel, as shown in the photo at left. The setup time is considerable but the jig offers some appealing advantages. Since the stock can be fed with the direction of cutter rotation (normally, an unsafe practice) the resulting cuts are extremely smooth with virtually no tearout. Also, work held in the left-hand clamp automatically adjusts work held in the right-hand clamp, so if you adjust the setting to cut the tails for a dovetail, for example, the pin adjustment is simultaneously indexed. The jig is also ideal for production-type operation; the dovetails for up to a dozen workpieces can be cut at the same time in a matter of a few minutes.

Incra Jig

The Incra is installed on a router table to replace the standard fence. It is simply screwed to a piece of plywood and then clamped to the table. The jig features fine adjustments that allow the fence to be shifted in precise increments —with an accessory, as fine as 0.001 inch. The Incra can be used to cut either dovetails or box joints, as shown at left.

with a higher price tag and usually involves more setup time than a fixed-template type of jig.

Most commercial jigs are designed to cut dovetails, since this joint is a cornerstone of cabinetmaking and one that seems tailor-made for the router to produce. There are also jigs for cutting mortise-and-tenons, like the MorTen shown on page 101, while some dovetail jigs, like the Leigh, can be adapted to cut both dovetails and mortise-and-tenons. Before buying a jig consider whether you need all the features that it provides. There is no point buying a device that requires an hour or two setup time if you only plan to cut a few joints. On the other hand, one big project may make the purchase of a jig pay for itself. A traditional six-board blanket chest, for example, requires more than 50 dovetails. Unless you are very experienced, those joints will take you hours— if not days—to cut by hand. A simple jig like the Keller, on the other hand, would enable you to do the job easily in a single morning.

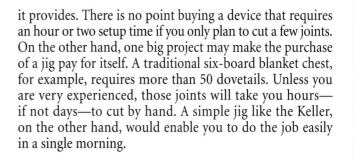

Keller Jig

The Keller is a simple, fixed-template dovetail jig, of which there are numerous varieties on the market. This particular device consists of two templates—one for cutting the pins and one for cutting the tails. The templates are mounted to backup boards and then clamped to the workpiece. A dovetail bit is used to cut the tails, as shown in the photo below, while a straight bit routs the pins. Each bit has a bearing that guides the router in and out of the jig's fingers to cut the joint. A stop-block (clamped to the right of the workpiece in the photo) makes it easy to cut any number of joints with the same setup. The jig is available in 12-inch and 24-inch models.

Leigh Dovetail Jig

The Leigh's distinctive feature is its finger assembly, which, as shown above, can be adjusted with a screwdriver to alter the spacing and width of the pins, giving a handcrafted look to the dovetails it helps cut. Once the pins are adjusted, the tails are set automatically. The finger assembly is simply flipped over to cut the mating part. The finger-guide assembly can be adjusted precisely to fine-tune the tightness of the joint. The jig can be used to cut a variety of dovetails, including through, half-blind, sliding, and outlined. An attachment also enables it to rout mortise-and-tenon joints. The jig is available in 12-inch and 24-inch models.

DOUBLE DADO JOINT

The double dado joint connects two dadoes, one dado on the inside face of one board and the other dado—with one tongue shortened—on the end of the mating piece. The joint is stronger than a standard through dado because it provides more gluing surface. It is an ideal choice for joining boards of different thicknesses, such as attaching a drawer front to the sides, and provides good resistance to tension and racking. The setup shown in the steps below and on the following page will join a ³/₄-inch-thick drawer front to a ¹/₂-inch-thick drawer side. The three cuts can all be made with the same bit—a three-wing slotting cutter. In this case, a ¹/₄-inch bit is used; the shim attached to the auxiliary fence is also ¹/₄ inch thick. By varying the sizes of the cutter and shim, you can cut the same joint in boards of different thicknesses.

ROUTING A DOUBLE DADO JOINT

1 Dadoing the ends of the drawer front
If you are using double dadoes to assemble a drawer, cut the dadoes with the shortened tongue on the ends of the drawer front. Start by installing a three-wing slotting cutter in a router and mounting the tool in a table. Cut a notch for the bit through an 8-inch-high auxiliary fence and attach the fence in place; the high fence is essential for feeding stock across the table on end *(steps 2 and 3)*. Position the fence in line with the outer edge of the bit pilot bearing and parallel to the miter slot, then set the cutting height by butting the workpiece against the bit and centering the cutter on the end of the board. Keeping the face of the board flat on the table and the end pressed against the fence, feed it into the cutter using the miter gauge *(right)*.

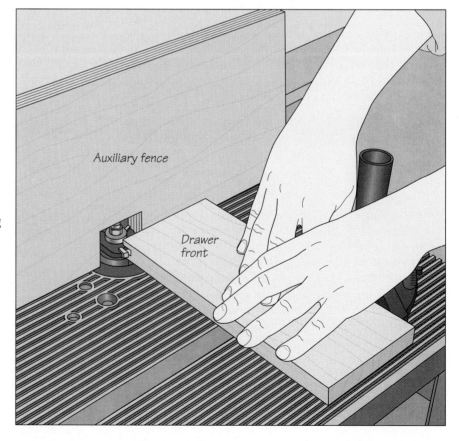

Auxiliary fence

Drawer front

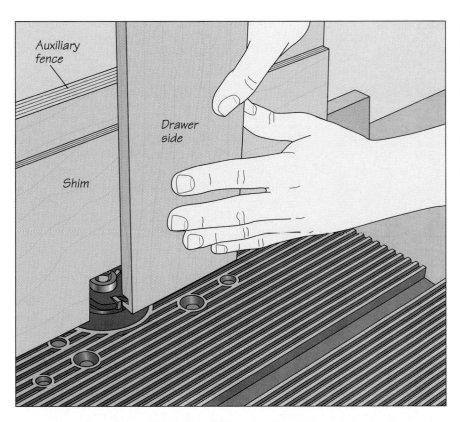

2 Dadoing the drawer side

Cut a notch in a wood shim for the cutter and screw it to the auxiliary fence. The shim should be as long as the fence and equal in thickness to the difference in thickness between the drawer front and sides. To rout the dado in the drawer side, hold its end flat on the table and its inside face flush against the shim as you feed it across the table *(left)*. Be sure to keep your hands clear of the cutter.

3 Trimming the inside tongues on the drawer front

To complete the joint, you need to shorten the inside tongue of each dado you routed in step 1. Lower the cutting height of the bit so the bottom edge of the cutter is just above the tabletop. Then feed the drawer front across the table as in step 2, holding the inside face against the shim *(below)*.

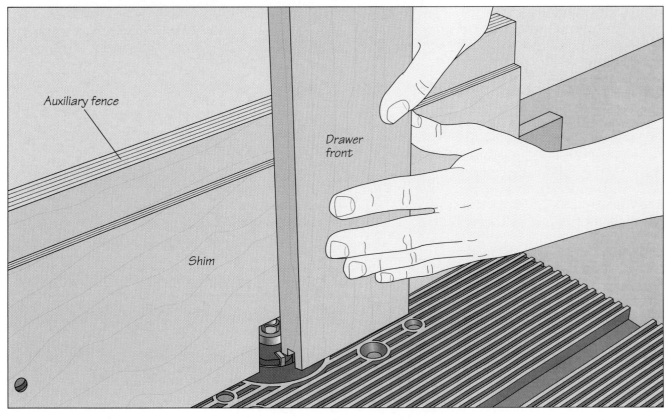

CORNER HALF-LAP JOINT

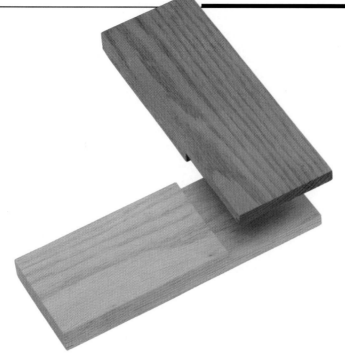

The corner half-lap joint is often used to assemble frames and doors. Adding dowels or screws to the joint provides an extra measure of strength. The joint can be cut on a table saw with a dado blade, but a router will do the job just as well. Do not try to make the cut freehand. This joint depends upon perfectly square shoulder cuts. Use a T-square like the one shown below to guide the router. If you are making many repeat cuts on boards that are the same size, take the time to build the jig shown on page 93.

ROUTING A CORNER HALF-LAP JOINT

Using a T-square jig

To rout half-laps with shoulders that are straight and square to the edges of the stock, use a T-square jig like the one shown at right. Make the jig from ¾-inch plywood so that each piece is about 4 inches wide; the fence should extend on either side of the edge guide by about the width of the router base plate. Assemble the jig by attaching the fence to the guide with countersunk screws, using a try square to make certain the two pieces are perpendicular to each other. Mark the shoulder of the half-lap on your workpiece and set the stock on a work surface. Install a straight bit in the router, align the cutter with the shoulder line of the half-lap, and clamp the jig atop the workpiece so the edge guide is butted against the router base plate, and the edges of the fence and workpiece are flush against each other. Rout the half-lap with a series of passes that run across the end of the stock, as shown by the arrow in the illustration. Start at the end of the workpiece and continue until you make the last pass with the router riding along the edge guide.

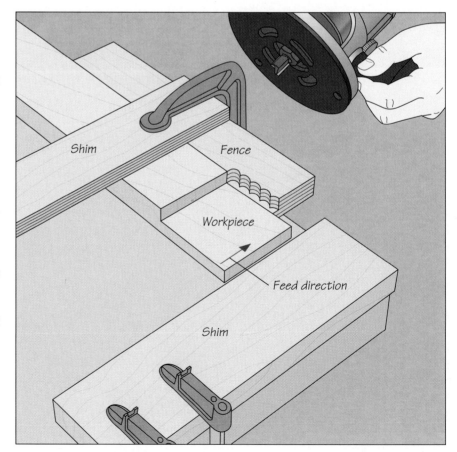

CORNER HALF-LAP JOINT JIG

If you have to make corner half-laps in several boards of the same size, it is worth taking the time to build the jig at right. Cut the two base pieces and the stop block from plywood that is the same thickness as your stock. The base pieces should be wide enough to support the router base plate as you cut the half-laps and mount the side and end guides. Use solid wood strips for the four edge guides.

To assemble the jig, mark the shoulder of the half-lap on one workpiece and set the board face-up on a work surface. Butt the base pieces against the edges of the board so the shoulder mark is near the middle of the base pieces. Install a straight bit in the router and align the cutter with the shoulder mark. Position one end guide across the base pieces and against the tool's base plate. Without

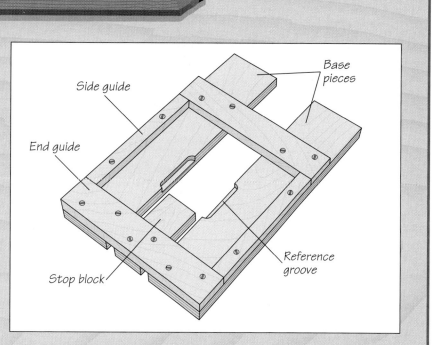

Side guide

End guide

Stop block

Base pieces

Reference groove

moving the workpiece, repeat the procedure to position the opposite guide. Now align the bit with the edges of the workpiece and attach the side guides, leaving a slight gap between the router base plate and each guide. (The first half-lap you make with the jig will rout reference grooves in the base pieces.) Slip the stop block under the end guide, butt it against the end of the workpiece, and screw it in place. Countersink all fasteners.

To use the jig, clamp it to the work surface and slide the workpiece between the base pieces until it butts against the stop block. Protecting the stock with a wood pad, clamp the workpiece in place. Adjust the router's cutting depth to one-half the stock thickness. Then, with the router positioned inside the guides, grip the tool firmly, turn it on, and lower the bit into the workpiece. Guide the router in a clockwise direction to cut the outside edges of the half-lap, keeping the base plate flush against a guide at all times. Then rout out the remaining waste *(left)*, feeding the tool against the direction of bit rotation.

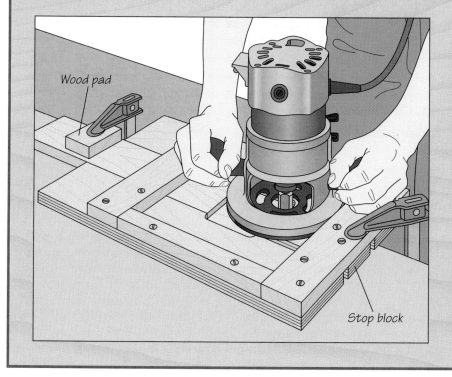

Wood pad

Stop block

PLATE JOINT

Fitted with a three-wing slotting cutter and mounted in a commercial biscuit joiner attachment, a router cuts semicircular slots for wood biscuits. Glued into two mating slots, the biscuits form a strong and durable plate joint—without the expense of a plate joiner. You can also cut the same joint on a router table with a simple shop-made setup, as shown below and on the following page. In fact, a table-mounted router can cut all the same joints as a biscuit joiner, including edge-to-edge, edge-to-face, and end-to-face joints. One exception is an edge-to-face joint in the middle of a panel, such as would typically be needed to install fixed shelves in a bookcase.

ROUTING BISCUIT SLOTS

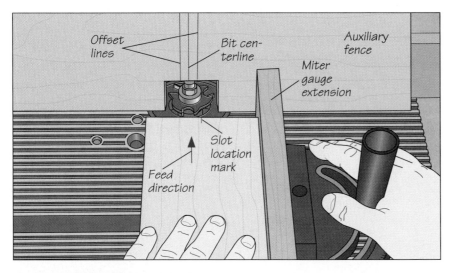

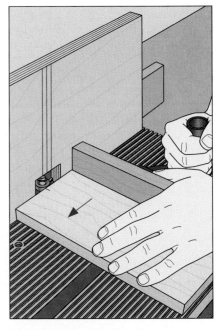

1 Plunging the workpiece into the bit
To rout biscuit slots for an end-to-face plate joint, as shown here and on page 95, start by slotting the end grain. Set up for the cut as you would for a double dado *(page 90)*, installing a three-wing slotting cutter in the router and an auxiliary fence on the router table. Also screw a board to the miter gauge as an extension. Since the wood biscuits are longer than the bit diameter, you will need to feed the workpiece along the fence after plunging the bit into the stock. Draw a line across the fence centered above the cutter and mark the slot location on the workpiece centered between the edges. Measure the difference between the biscuit length and cutter diameter, and mark lines on each side of the centerline on the fence, offsetting each one by one-half the measured difference. To start the slot, butt the edge of the workpiece against the miter gauge extension with the end clear of the bit and align the slot location mark with the offset line on the infeed side of the fence *(above)*. Then slide the board along the extension, plunging the end grain into the cutter.

2 Completing the slot
Once the board end is flush against the fence, slowly slide the miter gauge forward, holding the workpiece against both the extension and the fence *(above)*. Pivot the stock away from the fence—without lifting it off the table—once the slot location mark aligns with the offset line on the outfeed side of the fence.

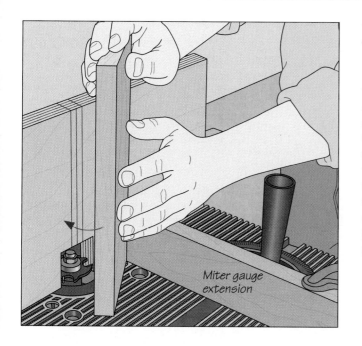

Miter gauge
extension

3 Slotting the face of the mating board

Mark the slot location on the inside face of the work-piece (near the top end so you can see the mark when the board is flush against the fence). Hold the workpiece against the fence with the location mark aligned with the offset line on the infeed side of the fence, then butt the miter gauge against the edge of the board and clamp it in place. With the workpiece clear of the cutter, turn on the router. Pressing the edge of the board against the miter gauge, pivot the inside face toward the fence *(left)*, plunging the bit into the stock. Once the board is flush against the fence, slowly slide it forward, keeping it pressed against the fence. Stop feeding the workpiece once the slot location mark aligns with the offset line on the outfeed side of the fence. Then turn off the router and pivot the board away from the fence.

BUILD IT YOURSELF

JIG FOR ROUTING BISCUIT SLOTS

The jig shown at right will enable you to rout slots for wood biscuits using a hand-held router fitted with a top-piloted ⁵⁄₃₂-inch three-wing slotting cutter. Make the jig base from ½-inch plywood—long enough to accommodate the three notches and wider than the router base plate diameter. Cut the notches into the edges of the base, one for each biscuit size. On one edge, make a 1¹¹⁄₁₆-inch-long notch for No. 20 biscuits and on the opposite edge, a 1⁷⁄₁₆-inch-long notch for No. 10 biscuits and a 1³⁄₁₆-inch-long notch for No. 0 biscuits. Cut all the notches 1 inch deep; label each one and mark its center. To position the base squarely on a workpiece, cut four 1-inch-wide edge guides and glue one in each corner of the base, two per face.

To rout a slot, set your stock on a work surface and clamp the jig on top, aligning the center mark of the

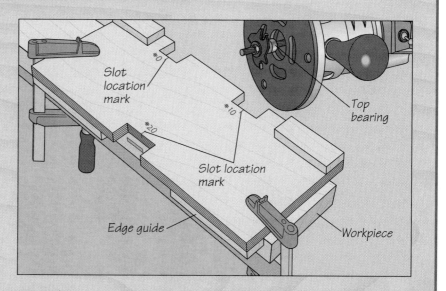

Slot location mark

Slot location mark

Top bearing

Edge guide

Workpiece

appropriate notch with the slot location mark on the workpiece. Make sure the edge guides on the underside of the base are flush against the stock. With the router base plate flat on the jig base and the bit clear of the workpiece, turn

on the router. Cut the slot by guiding the cutter along the bottom of the notch, starting with the pilot bearing pressed against one edge of the notch, riding it along the bottom and stopping when it contacts the opposite edge.

LOCK MITER JOINT

Also known as a drawer lock joint, the lock miter is often used to assemble drawers. The joint features identical cuts in the mating boards, one in a board end and the other along the joining face. Both cuts are produced on a router table with the same bit. Because the lock miter is suitable with plywood, it is a good alternative to dovetails in such situations.

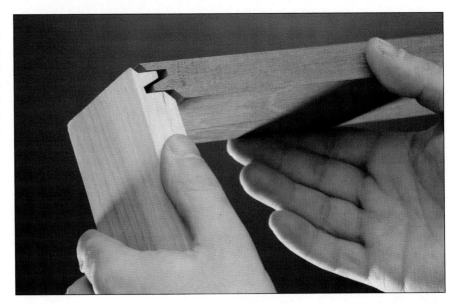

ROUTING A LOCK MITER

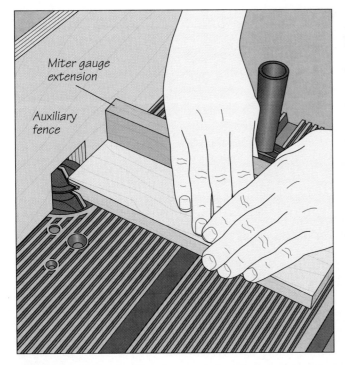

Making the cuts

Install a lock miter bit in your router and mount the tool in a table. Attach a notched auxiliary fence *(page 90)* and screw an extension board to the miter gauge. Set the bit height so the uppermost cutter is centered on the board end with the workpiece flat on the table. Position the fence so the bit will dado the stock without shortening it. Holding the workpiece against the fence and the miter gauge extension, feed the stock into the bit *(above, left)*. To cut the mating piece, clamp a guide block to it to ride along the top of the fence. Then feed the board on end into the cutter, keeping it flush against the fence with one hand while pushing it and the guide block forward with the other hand *(above, right)*.

MORTISE-AND-TENON JOINT

A tenon at the end of a table rail is fitted into a mortise in the leg shown at left. Since routers plow out a mortise with rounded corners, but cut a square tenon, some adjustment to the initial cut is necessary to ensure a snug-fitting joint. The corners of the mortise can be squared by hand with a chisel, as in the example illustrated here, or the edges of the tenon can be rounded over.

MAKING A MORTISE-AND-TENON WITH A ROUTER

1 Making the mortising jig
Assembled from ¾-inch plywood, the jig shown at right will help you rout mortises. Make the top and upright about 10 inches long and 6 inches wide. Cut an oval slot in the middle of the top, making it slightly longer than the mortise outline and wide enough to contain the outline and the template guide you will use with the bit. Screw the pieces together in a T shape, countersinking your fasteners; make the gap between the slot and the upright measure at least one-half the thickness of the thickest stock you plan to mortise. This will enable you to center the mortise outline under the slot with the board face flush against the upright; you can center thinner stock by placing shims between the workpiece and the upright.

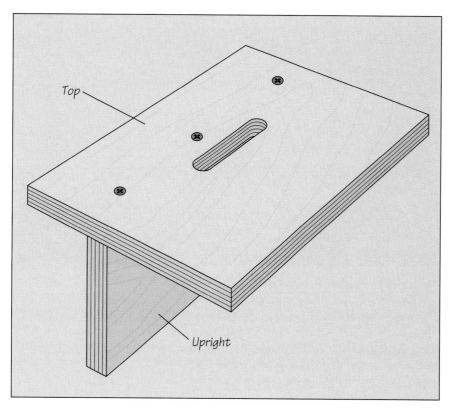

Top

Upright

2 Routing the mortise

Clamp the jig to the workpiece with the mortise outline centered under the slot; place shims between the workpiece and upright, if necessary. Secure the upright in a bench vise, setting a support board under the workpiece to hold it snug against the top. Install a ⅜-inch mortising bit in a plunge router, attach a template guide to the sub-base, and adjust the cutting depth so you can rout the mortise in two or three successively deeper passes *(right)*. Hold the router flat on the jig top with the bit centered over one end of the slot. Turn on the tool and plunge the bit into the stock. Then feed the tool to the other end of the slot to finish the cut, pressing the template guide against the inside edge of the slot throughout the procedure.

Support board

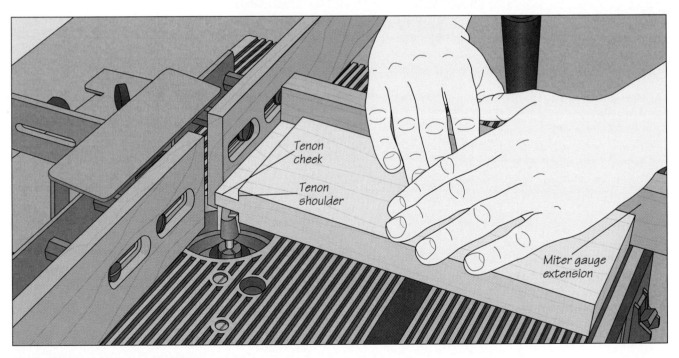

Tenon cheek

Tenon shoulder

Miter gauge extension

3 Cutting the tenon on a router table

Mount the router in a table, screw an extension board to the miter gauge, and mark the tenon shoulders on the workpiece, using the finished mortise as a guide. Adjust the cutting width so the gap between the fence and the bit equals the distance between the shoulder line and the end of the board. Set the cutting height to obtain a tenon slightly thicker than the mortise you cut in Step 2. Butting the rail against the fence and the miter gauge extension, feed the workpiece face down into the cutter. Turn the board over and repeat to cut the other tenon cheek *(above)*. Test-fit the thickness of the tenon in the mortise and make additional passes until the fit is snug. Then mark the top and bottom of the tenon on the cheek, adjust the bit height to cut to the line and feed the stock on edge, making a pass on each edge to complete the tenon.

Workpiece

Feed direction

V-block jig

4 Rounding over the tenons

One way to ensure that a square-edged tenon fits snugly in a router-made mortise—with its rounded corners—is to round over the edges of the tenon, using either your table saw or a shop knife. For the table saw method, cut a V-shaped wedge out of a wood block, creating a jig that will hold the workpiece at an angle to the saw blade. Position the jig on the table alongside the blade, slide the miter gauge up against the jig, and clamp the gauge in place. Screw the jig to the miter gauge. Adjust the cutting height so the blade will just trim the corner of the tenon. The rip fence should be positioned so the saw blade will not cut into the tenon shoulder. Then turn on the saw and, holding the face of the workpiece flush against one side of the V, slide the stock along the jig (as shown by the arrow in the illustration) until it touches the fence, trimming the corner of the tenon. Reposition the workpiece in the jig to trim the remaining tenon corners *(above, left)*. For the shop knife method, simply round over the tenon by trimming the corners from the end of the board to the shoulder *(above, right)*.

SHOP TIP

A round-tenon jig for the router table

The simple plywood jig shown here enables you to rout round tenons in turned pieces. Make the L-shaped jig higher than your router table's fence, with a brace that holds the workpiece snugly. Install a straight bit in the router and an insert in the table that surrounds the cutter as closely as possible. Adjust the cutter height to the length of the tenon. Then clamp the jig to the center of the fence and set them for a partial cut. Holding the workpiece securely in the jig with one hand, turn on the router and lower the stock onto the bit while turning it clockwise, against bit rotation. Advance the fence ⅛ inch at a time until the tenon is completed.

TWO WAYS TO ROUT MORTISES

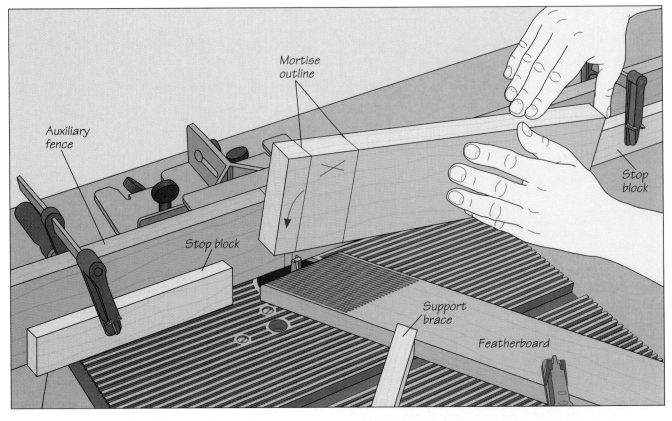

Routing a mortise on a router table with twin stop blocks

Mount your router in a table with a mortising bit in the tool. The bit's diameter should be equal to the mortise width—typically, about one-third the stock thickness. Mark the beginning and end of the mortise on all four sides of the workpiece, then center an end of the board on the bit and butt an auxiliary fence against the stock. Clamp a featherboard to the table, bracing it with a support board clamped at a 90° angle to its edges; round over the top corner of the featherboard slightly to facilitate lowering the workpiece onto the bit. To help you determine the location of the cutter when it is hidden by the workpiece during this cut, mark the points on the fence where the bit starts and stops cutting. Next, align the mortise start line on the workpiece with the bit, butt a stop block against the bottom end of the stock and clamp it to the infeed side of the fence. Then align the mortise end line with the bit, butt a second stop block against the top end of the workpiece, and clamp it in place. Turn on the router and lower the workpiece onto the bit, keeping it flush against the fence and the infeed-side stop block *(above)*. Feed the workpiece across the table, pressing the stock against the fence and flat on the table *(right)*. Once the workpiece contacts the stop block on the outfeed side of the fence, turn off the router.

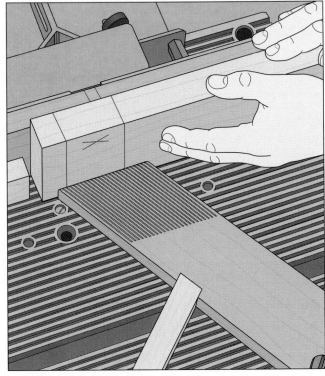

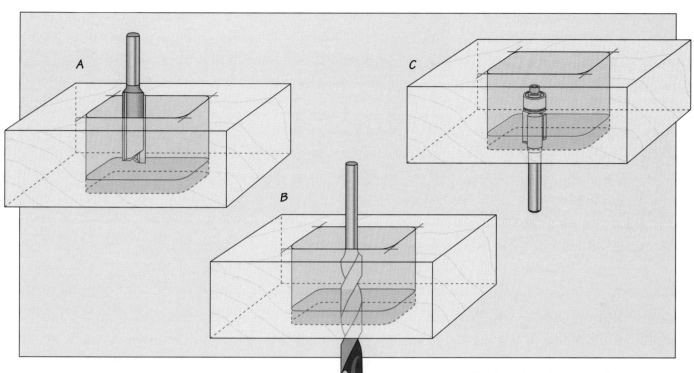

Routing a deep through mortise

If the desired depth of a mortise exceeds your router's maximum depth of cut, use an electric drill to help cut the cavity. The illustration above shows the three steps necessary to cut a mortise through thick stock. Start by installing a mortising bit in the router and making as many passes as you can until you can go no deeper **(A)**. Then use the drill with a bit that is larger than your router bit to bore a hole through the remaining waste **(B)**. Install a piloted flush-trimming bit in the router and turn the workpiece over. Inserting the bit through the hole made by the drill, rout out the waste **(C)**; keep the pilot bearing pressed against the walls of the mortise to complete the cut. Use a chisel to square the mortise corners, if desired.

Clamped in a bench vise, a commercial mortise-and-tenon jig guides a router as it cuts a tenon. The jig template is turned end-for-end to rout the matching mortise.

POCKET HOLES

A laminate trimmer slides along a shop-built jig to rout a recess, or "pocket," for a screw in the face frame rail shown at right. Pocket holes are commonly used with screws for joining face frame members or attaching a tabletop to its supporting rails. Because they recess the fasteners below the surface of the workpiece, pocket holes solve the problem of having to screw straight through 3- or 4-inch-wide stock; they also conceal the fasteners. The jig shown, designed by Patrick Spielman, features a slot that allows a laminate trimmer to rout the screw recesses.

USING A SHOP-MADE JIG

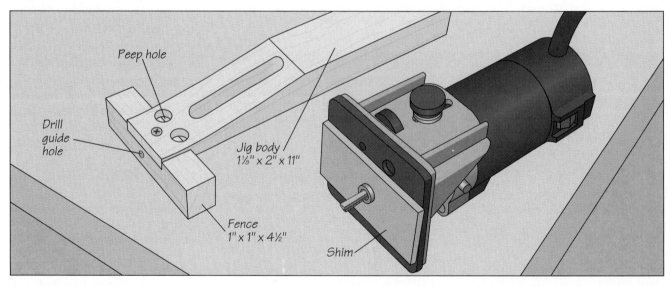

1 Making the pocket-hole jig

Cut the jig body and fence from hardwood, then taper the top face of the body in a gentle concave curve, starting the cut 5 inches from one end. Now rout a ½-inch-wide, 3½-inch-long slot through the body, centered on the tapered face, as shown above. Drill two peep holes through the body near the tapered end; the holes will help you align the workpiece with the jig. Notch the top of the fence to accommodate the body, then glue the pieces together so the end of the body is flush with the outside edge of the fence. Once the adhesive has cured, bore the ³⁄₁₆-inch-diameter guide hole through the fence; align the bit with the slot in the body as you drill the hole. Screw the body to the fence, making sure the fastener does not intersect with the guide hole. Finally, drive two brads into the inside edge of the fence, leaving their heads protruding, then snip off the heads with pliers; the pointed ends of the brads will help you position the workpiece against the fence. To prepare the laminate trimmer for the jig, cut a narrow shim from ¼-inch hardboard as long as the tool base is wide, drill a hole through it for the bit and template guide *(step 2)* you will use, and fix it to the base of the trimmer with double-sided tape. (The shim will allow the router to ride smoothly along the slightly curved surface of the taper.)

2 Routing the pocket

Install a cutter and template guide in the laminate trimmer; the cutter diameter should be slightly greater than the heads of the screws you will be using to join the workpieces. Then set the stock on a work surface, place the pocket-hole jig on top and, with the brads securing the workpiece flush against the fence, clamp the assembly in place. Holding the trimmer above the jig with the bit centered over one end of the slot, turn on the tool and plunge the bit into the stock until the hardboard shim is flat on the jig body. Then feed the tool along the jig to the other end of the slot to finish the cut, pressing the template guide against the inside edges of the slot through the cut *(right)*.

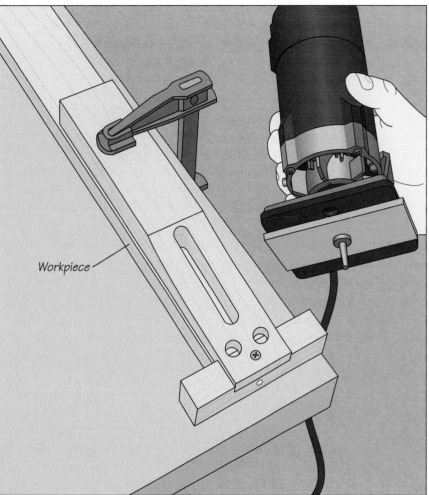

Workpiece

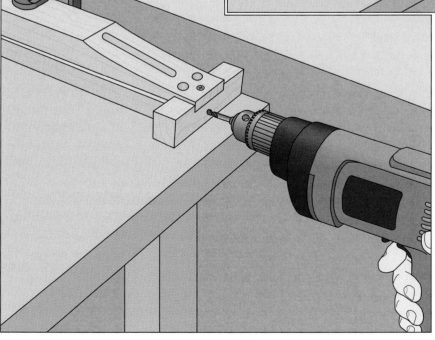

3 Drilling the pilot hole

To complete the pocket hole, you need to drill the pilot hole for the screw used to secure the joint. Fit the bit into the guide hole in the jig fence and bore the hole *(left)*. The bit should emerge from the top of the workpiece, centered in the pocket you routed in step 2.

DOVETAIL JOINTS

Combining enduring strength with an attractive apperance, the through dovetail is often used in fine furniture to join carcase corners. The half-blind version of the joint shown starting on page 108 is a good choice for assembling drawers because the drawer front conceals the end grain of the sides. Traditionally, the joint was cut using a handsaw and chisel, but many woodworkers now make it with a router. There are a raft of jigs on the market that, paired with a router, enable you to cut a variety of dovetail joints (page 88). But you can also make them by using the techniques shown in this section, producing both through and half-blind dovetails.

CUTTING THROUGH DOVETAILS ON A ROUTER TABLE

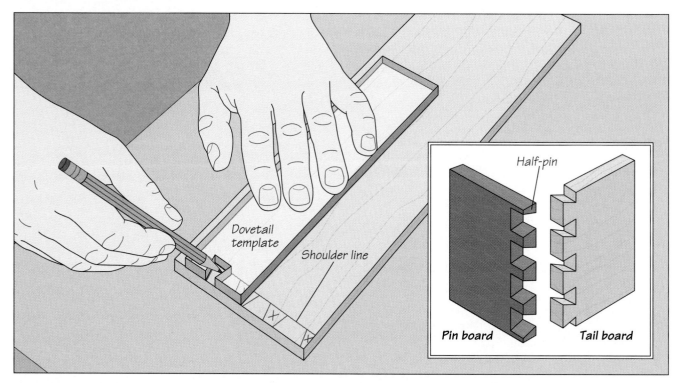

Dovetail template

Shoulder line

Half-pin

Pin board   Tail board

1 Marking the tails with a shop-made template

A dovetail joint consists of a tail board and a pin board with half-pins at each end *(inset)*. To rout the joint, start by using a cutting gauge adjusted to the stock thickness to scribe a shoulder line across one end of the tail board. To mark the tails, use a shop-made template; cut a piece of clear acrylic plastic about 3 inches wide and 8 inches long, then rout a notch into one end with the same dovetail bit you will use to cut the joint. The size and shape of the notch will correspond to the waste sections between the tails—that is, the pins. Set the tail board on a work surface, position the template on top, and start by marking waste sections equal to one-half the notch width at each edge; be sure to align the template's notched end with the board end and hold its edges parallel to those of the workpiece. Outline the remaining waste sections *(above)*, marking them with an x as you go. There are no rigid guidelines for the number of tails required, but evenly spaced tails that are at least twice the size of the waste sections between them produce an attractive and sturdy joint.

2 Routing away the waste from the tail board edges

Mount your router in a table with the bit used to notch the dovetail template and screw an extension board to the miter gauge. Securing the tail board on end, adjust the cutting height so the bit will cut to the shoulder line. Then align one of the waste sections at the edge of the board with the bit and clamp the work-piece to the extension. Butt a stop block against an edge of the board and secure it to the extension so you can rout the waste sections at each corner of the board using the same setup. To cut the first waste section, slide the miter gauge forward. Then turn the board around, butt it against the stop block, reclamp the workpiece to the extension and repeat the cut. Cut the waste sections at the other end of the board the same way *(right)*.

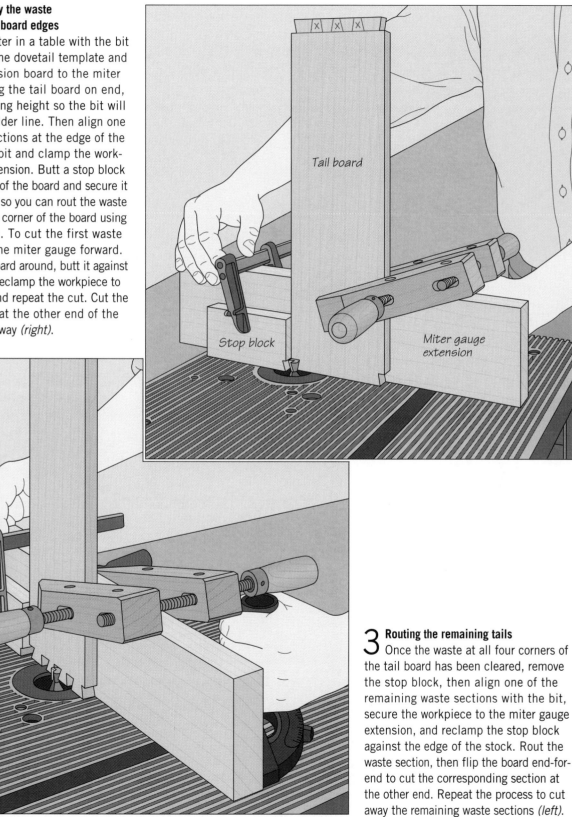

Tail board

Stop block

Miter gauge extension

3 Routing the remaining tails

Once the waste at all four corners of the tail board has been cleared, remove the stop block, then align one of the remaining waste sections with the bit, secure the workpiece to the miter gauge extension, and reclamp the stop block against the edge of the stock. Rout the waste section, then flip the board end-for-end to cut the corresponding section at the other end. Repeat the process to cut away the remaining waste sections *(left)*.

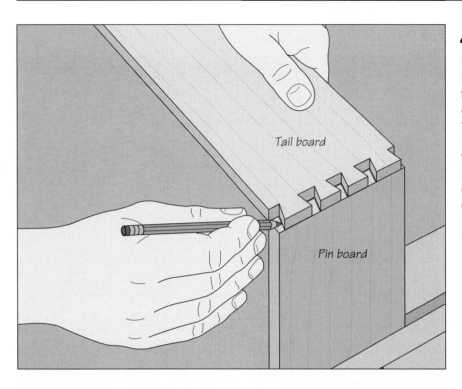

Tail board

Pin board

4 Marking the pins
Secure the pin board end-up in a bench vise and hold the completed tail board in position across the end. Making sure the edges of the two boards are aligned and the end of the tail board is flush with the outside face of the pin board, run a pencil along each edge of the tails to outline the pins on the end of the pin board *(left)*. Extend all the pin marks down both faces of the board, using a combination square to ensure that the lines are perpendicular to the end of the board. Mark each waste section with an X.

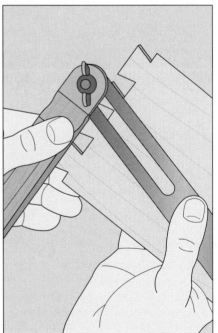

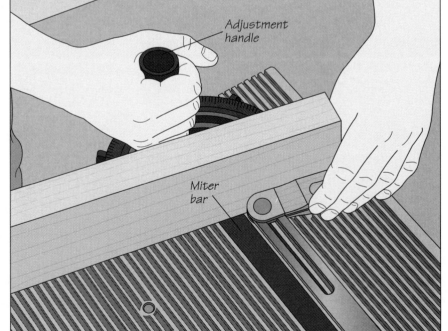

Adjustment handle

Miter bar

5 Adjusting the router table miter gauge
Since the pins are wider on the inside face of the board, you need to angle the miter gauge on your router table when you cut them *(steps 6 and 7)*. To determine the correct angle, use a sliding bevel. Holding the handle of the device flush against the end of the tail board, adjust the blade to align with the edge of one of the tails *(above, left)*. Then loosen the adjustment handle on the router table miter gauge, butt the handle of the sliding bevel against the gauge extension, and swivel the head of the gauge until the blade of the sliding bevel is parallel to the miter bar *(above, right)*. Tighten the adjustment handle.

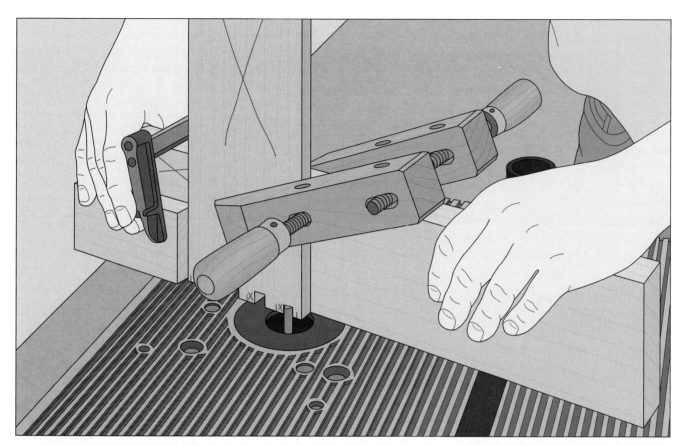

SHOP TIP

**Dealing with a
defective dovetail**
Even a slight error
in cutting dove-
tails can result
in a small gap
between a pin
and a tail. If the gap is
small, fill it with a thin
triangular chip of veneer or a wood
shaving cut from the panel stock. To
make the wood chip less obvious, cut it
so that its grain will run in the same
direction as that of the pins. Use a dovetail
saw to straighten out or deepen the gap, if
necessary. Apply a little glue in the gap and
insert the chip, which should fit snugly.

6 **Routing the right-hand edge of the pins**
Install a straight bit in the router and
adjust the cutting depth to slightly more
than the thickness of the tail board. Align
the right-hand edge of the first marked
waste section with the bit, butt a stop
block against the edge of the stock and
clamp it to the miter gauge extension.
Holding the extension with both hands,
feed the workpiece into the bit. Then turn
the stock end-for-end, clamp it to the
extension with its edge flush against the
stop block, and repeat the cut at the other end of the board. Move the stop block
away from the bit by an amount equal to
the cutter diameter and make another cut
at each end of the board, continuing until
you have cleared at least one-half the
waste; do not rout away much more than
half the waste, or you risk cutting into the
neighboring pins. Repeat the process for
each waste section *(above)*, shifting the
stop block as necessary.

7 Routing the remaining waste from the pin board

Once you have cut away half the waste from the pin board, remove the workpiece and stop block, and use the sliding bevel to angle the miter gauge in the opposite direction. Then follow the same procedure used in the previous step to clear the remaining stock from each waste section *(right)*.

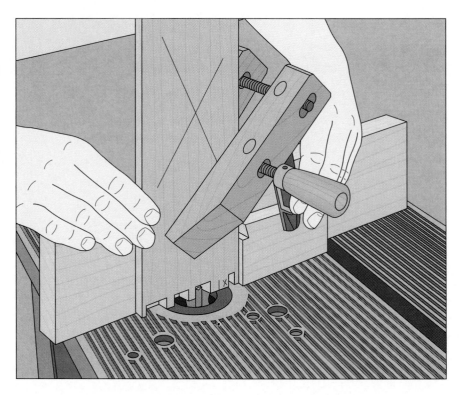

ROUTING HALF-BLIND DOVETAILS

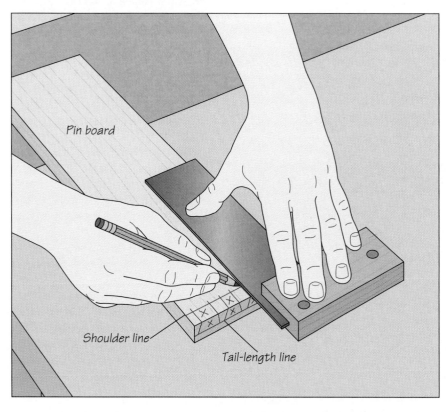

Pin board

Shoulder line

Tail-length line

1 Marking the pins

Start by cutting the tails on your router table, as described on page 104; with half-blind dovetails, adjust the cutting height so the length of the tails equals two-thirds the thickness of the pin board. Before outlining the pins, set a cutting gauge to the tail length and use it to mark a line across the end of the pin board, closer to the outside than the inside face. Adjust the cutting gauge to the thickness of the tail board and scribe a shoulder line on the inside face of the pin board. Then use the tail board as a guide to outline the pins on the end of the pin board *(page 106)*, but instead of lining up the ends of the tails with the outside face of the pin board, align them with the tail-end line. To complete the marking, use a try square and a pencil to extend the lines on the board end to the shoulder line *(left)*. Mark the waste sections with an x as you go.

2 Routing out the waste between the pins

Secure the pin board end-up in a bench vise and use a laminate trimmer fitted with a straight bit and an offset base to remove the waste from the workpiece. The offset base allows you to focus the downward pressure on the bench, which will help keep the tool from wobbling as you rout the waste. Screw a support board to a plywood shim and clamp the assembly in a vise with the workpiece. Adjust the stock up or down until the tip of the bit aligns with the shoulder line when the trimmer sits flat on the shim. Next, to keep from cutting beyond the tail-end line on the end of the pin board, align the bit with the line, butt an edge guide against the trimmer base, and secure the guide in place. Then, starting at one edge of the workpiece, rout out the waste between the pins *(right)*, keeping the trimmer flat on the shim throughout the operation. To avoid gouging the pins, cut only to within 1/16 inch of their marked edges.

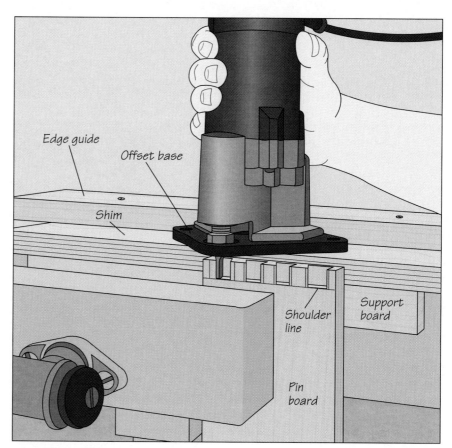

Edge guide

Offset base

Shim

Shoulder line

Support board

Pin board

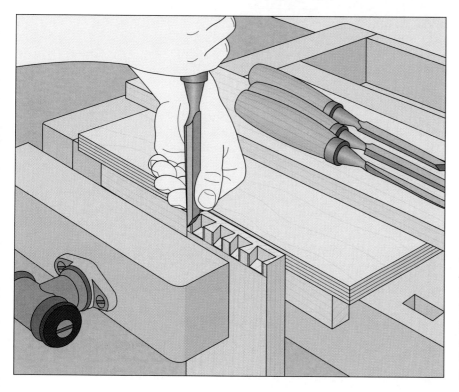

3 Final paring

Remove the remaining waste from the pin board with paring and skew chisels. Working on one waste section at a time, press the flat side of the chisel against the edges of the pins with a thumb and push the chisel toward the shoulder line, paring away the last slivers of waste *(left)*.

DECORATIVE TECHNIQUES

Although many wood-workers rank their routers high among the shop work-horses, the tools are capable of much more than simply shaping edges, plowing grooves, and routing circles. Paired with the appropriate jigs—whether commercial or shop-made—the router can accomplish a host of decorative tasks. This chapter will show you how to put jigs to work to expand your router's capabilities from the workaday to the more ornamental.

Fitted with a 60° V-bit and mounted in a table, for example, a router can cut precise wood threads *(page 117)*, enabling you to make items like handscrews or vises in the shop. As shown on page 114, the same result can be achieved with a router and a commercial wood threader. And with a shop-made jig you can use a table-mounted router to make dowels from hardwood stock *(page 118)*.

The router can also be used to shape and adorn furniture parts with the precision and artfulness usually restricted to

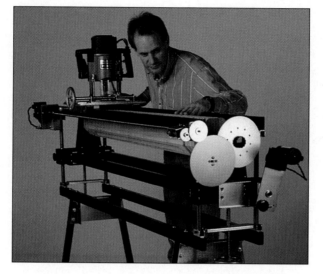

The commercial milling machine shown above transforms the router into a carving tool. Much like a lathe, the machine secures up to three workpieces between centers. Fixed to a metal plate, a router can then be fed along the bed of the machine by hand or with a motor drive. The router can also be left stationary while the crank is turned at the other end of the machine, rotating the workpiece into the bit.

carving tools in practised hands. Coupled with a simple shop-made jig and a pair of clamps, the router can taper legs *(page 119)*. And, as shown in the photo at left, you can rout flutes into lathe-mounted quarter columns using the simple jig shown beginning on page 120. Other carving-like tasks include reeding turned legs *(page 123)*, spiraling legs *(page 125)*, carving decorative fans *(page 127)* and turned objects such as bowls *(page 130)*.

Although most router work is guided by jigs, freehand routing has its place. You can cut relief designs on wood panels *(page 136)* and etch lettering *(page 138)*. Even if you have the carving skills to accomplish some of these tasks by hand, one advantage of using the router is that the work will go more quickly. With speed, however, comes dust and noise. Be sure your shop has good ventilation and dust collection, and wear a dust mask, hearing protection, and safety goggles for all routing operations.

Fastened to a box-like jig that rides along the bed of a lathe, the router shown at left plows a flute in a quarter column. For instructions on building and using this jig, refer to page 120.

JIGS & EQUIPMENT FOR DECORATIVE WORK

COMMERCIAL JIGS AND ACCESSORIES

Pantograph
Allows router to carve copies of three-dimensional patterns (page 132)

Laminate trimmer
Lightweight enough to be used in free-hand routing (page 134)

Wood threader and tap
Used with a router to carve wood threads in cylindrical stock (page 114)

Turning jig
Converts a router into a fluting tool. As on a lathe, stock is mounted on the jig between centers; router is fastened to a metal platform. Turning the crank rotates the workpiece and moves router platform along a guide rail, enabling the cutter to shape the stock along its length. The height of the platform is adjustable to set cutting depth of bit

Some joint-making jigs go well beyond the merely functional and allow a router to create joints that give equal weight to decoration and strength. The device shown at left enables a router to cut both mating pieces of a pin-and-crescent joint.

Dowel-making jig
Used with router to make dowels from hardwood stock

SHOP-MADE JIGS

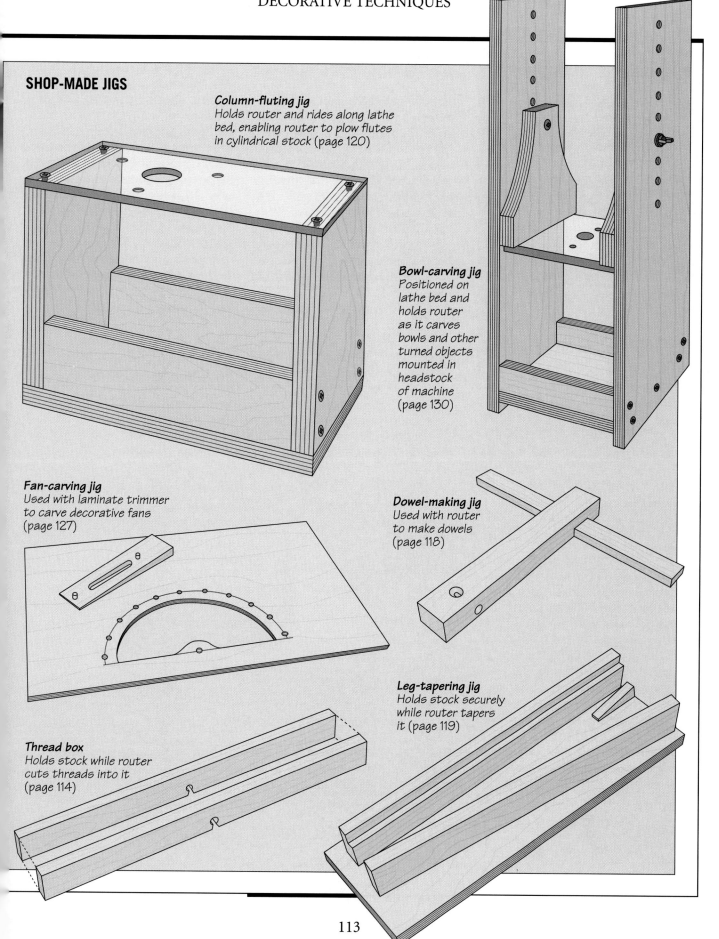

Column-fluting jig
Holds router and rides along lathe bed, enabling router to plow flutes in cylindrical stock (page 120)

Bowl-carving jig
Positioned on lathe bed and holds router as it carves bowls and other turned objects mounted in headstock of machine (page 130)

Fan-carving jig
Used with laminate trimmer to carve decorative fans (page 127)

Dowel-making jig
Used with router to make dowels (page 118)

Leg-tapering jig
Holds stock securely while router tapers it (page 119)

Thread box
Holds stock while router cuts threads into it (page 114)

DOWELS AND WOODEN THREADS

Making your own dowels provides for a great deal more flexibility in your woodworking projects than if you rely solely on commercial dowel stock. The principal advantage of custom-made dowels is that you can use any species—one that matches the surrounding wood or one that contrasts. Another benefit is that you can size the dowels precisely to suit your needs. The simple shop-built jig shown on page 118 describes how to use a router to transform square stock into dowels.

Woodworkers have been cutting wood threads for more than 2,000 years. The Romans used wooden screws in presses for olive oil and for wine. For the modern woodworker, wood threads have more pedestrian uses— in screws and bolts to embellish furniture or in shop-made clamps and vises. (See the front endpaper for instructions on making wooden handscrews.) The traditional method for creating wood threads involved handcutting them using a triangular file. Nowadays, as shown on the following pages, you can do the job much more quickly and easily by cutting threads on dowel stock with your router. Be sure to use a freshly sharpened bit; a dull cutter will strip the threads as it forms them.

Teamed up with a router, the commercial wood threader shown at left transforms a dowel into a wooden screw. The plastic sleeve holding the dowel determines the thread pitch while the metal plate holds the router upright, enabling its bit to cut the threads. A base was attached to the vertical support so the jig could be secured between bench dogs; the handle was also added to facilitate rotating the dowel.

ROUTING WOOD THREADS

1 Planning the job

Screws and bolts are sized to fit into an opening—a pilot hole, a plastic anchor or, as shown at right, a nut. When cutting threads into round stock, certain dimensions are critical. The high points of the threads, known as the crests, and the low points, or valleys, must complement the shape of the nut, although the crests in a wooden screw are flatter than they would be in a metal screw. In addition, the distance between adjoining crests, called the pitch of the thread, must be a perfect match between the fastener and the nut. Wooden screws are often categorized according to the diameters around their crests (major screw diameter) and around their valleys (minor screw diameter).

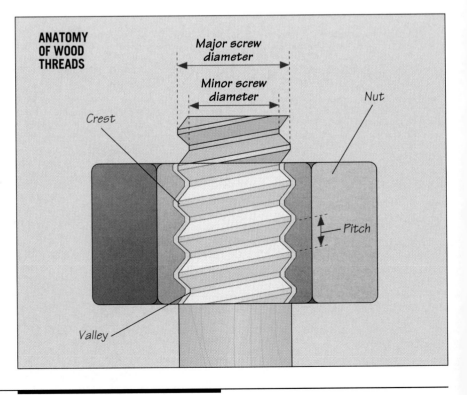

ANATOMY OF WOOD THREADS

Major screw diameter

Minor screw diameter

Crest

Nut

Pitch

Valley

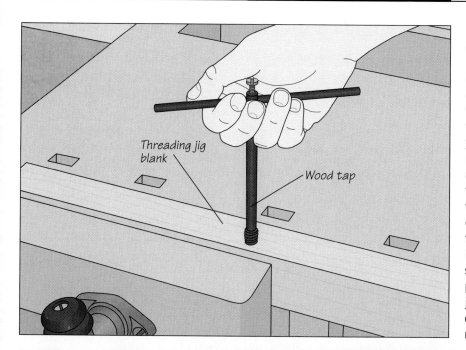

Threading jig blank

Wood tap

2 Tapping a feed hole

To rout threads into round stock, you need to prepare a threading jig. As shown on page 117, the jig will guide the dowel stock into the router bit, allowing the cutters to carve the threads. Start with a wood tap the same diameter as the threads you want; a ½-inch tap is shown in the illustration at left. Secure your jig blank—a 2-by-3 board will do fine—face-up in a vise and use the tap to cut threads all the way through the stock *(left)*. To feed the dowel stock into the jig, you need to enlarge the feed hole for about one-half its length. Install a bit in your drill press that is slightly larger than the feed hole, then position the hole under the bit, clamp the jig to the machine table, and adjust the drilling depth to one-half the stock thickness. Bore the hole *(below)*.

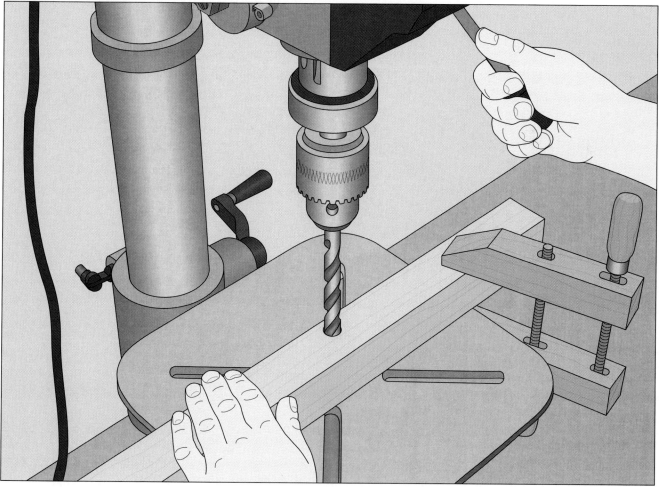

3 Preparing the threading jig for the router
With the threaded jig on edge on the router table, as shown below, the tip of the bit you will use should just reach the bottom edge of the feed hole. Use your band saw to notch the jig for the bit, making two 60° angle cuts from the bottom edge of the stock that intersect at the center of the feed hole *(right)*. The notch should be slightly larger than the bit. Mark the outside faces of the jig, then rip the board in half, separating the threaded portion of the feed hole from the unthreaded part; the cut is represented by the dotted lines in the illustration. Feed the cut face of each piece across a planer to flatten the surfaces, and make as many passes as necessary with the threaded portion until the crest of the first thread starts at the bottom of the V notch. This ensures that the jig will function properly.

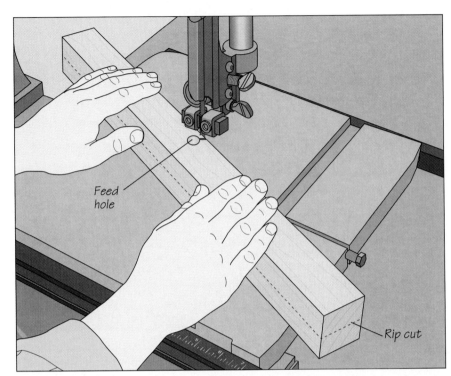

Feed hole

Rip cut

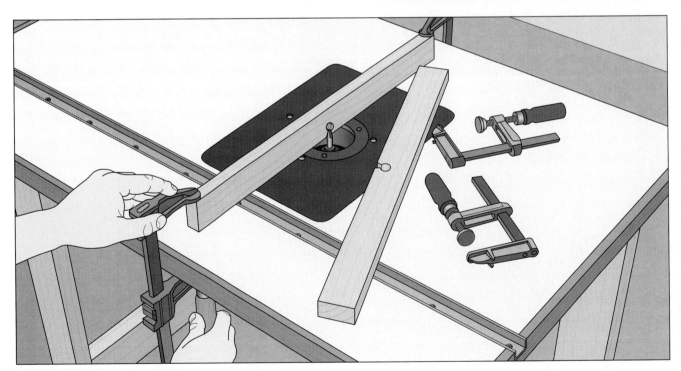

4 Installing the jig on the router table
Install a 60° V bit in the router and mount the tool in a table. Clamp the threaded half of the jig bottom-edge down to the table so the tip of the bit is just in front of the thread *(above)*. Adjust the router's cutting height so the tip of the bit is level with the crest of the thread in the jig. Butt the unthreaded half of the jig against the half already in place, align the holes, and clamp it in place. Make sure the marked faces of both pieces face out.

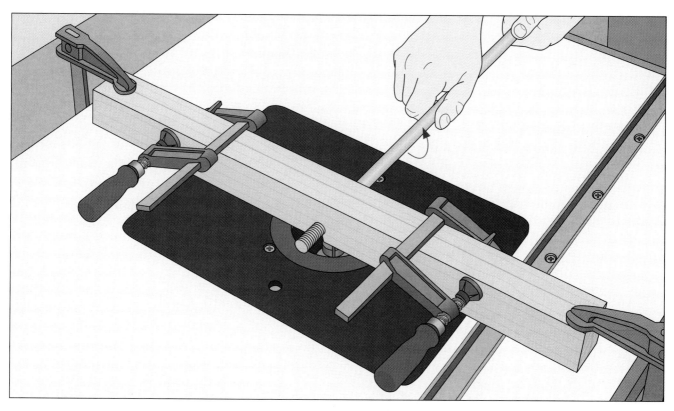

The handle is shown in use on page 114.

5 Cutting the thread
Turn on the router and slip the dowel into the unthreaded end of the feed hole. Push the dowel forward and once the cutter bites into the stock begin rotating the dowel in a clockwise direction, as indicated by the arrow in the illustration above. Continue until the dowel has been threaded to the desired length.

SHOP TIP

Making a handle to rotate dowels
To simplify the task of feeding dowel stock into a threading jig, fashion a turning handle. Cut a 2-by-2 piece of fine-grained hardwood about 10 inches long and drill a hole through it near each end. Make the holes the same diameter as the dowel stock you will be threading. Into one of the holes, glue a 5-inch-length of dowel as a handhold. Bore a third hole into an adjoining edge between the second hole and the end of the board; this third hole will accommodate a screw that secures the dowel to be threaded to the handle. Also cut a kerf from the end of the piece to the second hole to make it easier to tighten dowel stock in the handle. To use the handle, slip the dowel stock into the second hole and secure it by tightening a wing nut on the screw. The handle is shown in use on page 114.

A DOWEL-MAKING JIG

Teamed up with an electric drill and a table-mounted router fitted with a ½-inch straight bit, the jig shown at right can transform square stock into a dowel. The jig enables you to rotate the stock past a router bit that cuts away the waste. Cut the arm from a 2-by-3 piece of hardwood to a length of about 20 inches, then drill the bit clearance hole near one end through the face, making it slightly larger than the router bit diameter. Bore the feed holes in two steps. Start by drilling a hole through the edge of the arm that slightly overlaps the bit clearance hole; the diameter of the hole should equal the finished diameter of the dowel stock you want. Then switch to a larger drill bit and widen the infeed side of the hole enough to insert the square stock you will be using; stop drilling when you reach the bit clearance hole. Make sure the infeed hole is centered over the outfeed hole. Finally, cut a dado across the bottom face

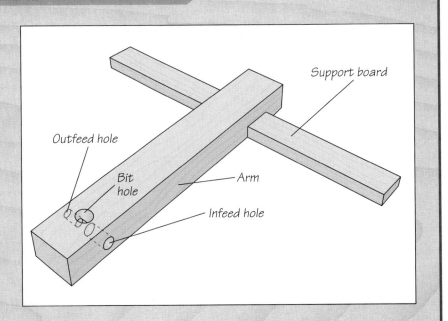

of the arm to accommodate the support board.

To use the jig, set the arm on the router table, centering the bit clearance hole over the cutter. Slip the support board into the dado in the arm and clamp the board parallel to the table end. Whittle one end of the square stock so you can tighten it securely in the chuck of an electric drill. Turn on the router and the drill, then feed the spinning stock into the infeed hole in the arm. As the router bit removes the waste, the dowel stock will emerge from the outfeed hole *(below)*.

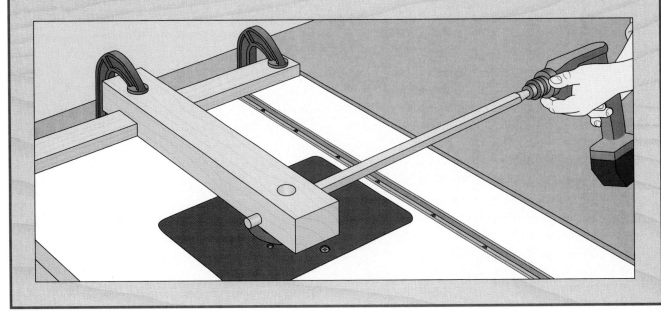

ROUTING DECORATIVE ACCENTS

Fluted quarter columns add a touch of elegance to the Queen Anne highboy shown above. The flutes were cut by a router using the jig and technique illustrated on page 120.

Carved accents and ornamentation have been a feature of fine furniture for centuries. Traditionally, these details were etched with painstaking skill by master carvers wielding a battery of gouges, chisels and files. While a router cannot duplicate the finely detailed work of a skilled carver, it can still produce impressive results with far less effort and training. With the right setup and techniques you can use your router to perform a variety of decorative cuts, from tapering legs and cutting flutes in quarter columns to shell carving. The flutes shown in the quarter column in the photo at left, for example, were cut in a cylinder while it was still mounted on a lathe; the router was fixed to a simple jig that rides along the lathe bed. Instructions for setting up the operation are shown beginning on page 120.

TAPERING A LEG

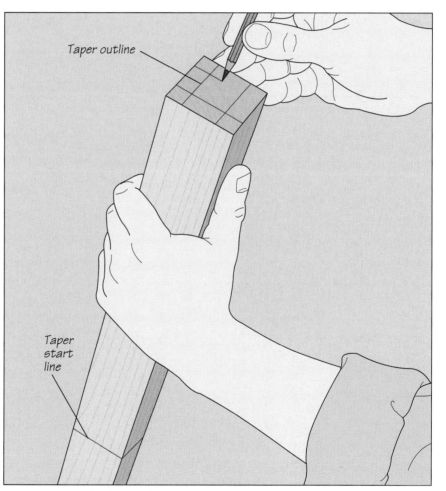

Taper outline

Taper start line

1 Marking the taper
Mark a line all around the leg near the top end to indicate where the taper should start, leaving enough space between the line and the top end for the joinery method you will use to attach the leg to the rails. Then outline the finished size of the taper on the bottom end, using your fingers as a guide to draw a line parallel to each edge of the stock *(above)*.

A COLUMN-FLUTING JIG

The jig shown at right will enable you to use a router for cutting flutes on your lathe turnings. Cut the pieces of the jig from ¾-inch plywood, except for the top, which is made from ¼-inch clear acrylic. The jig should be long and wide enough to support your router's base plate, and high enough to hold the tool just above the blank when the jig is set on the lathe bed.

Assemble the top, bottom, and sides of the jig, then add the braces for rigidity. Install a double-bearing piloted fluting bit in your router, bore a bit clearance hole through the jig top, and screw the tool's base plate to the jig.

To space the flutes equally, mark them on a faceplate. If you want 12 flutes, for example, divide 360 (the number of degrees in a circle) by 12, yielding a space of 30°. Use a protractor and a pencil to mark lines on the faceplate 30° apart *(below)*.

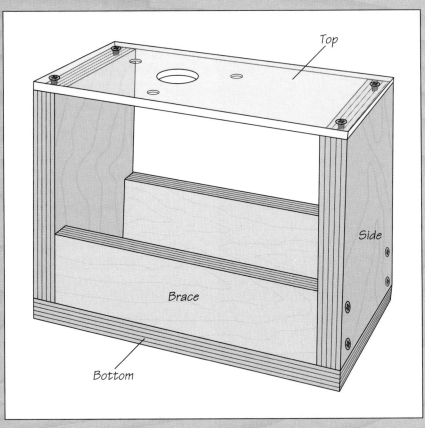

Flute line

Attach the faceplate to the headstock of the lathe.

To set up the jig, place it on the lathe bed and mount the blank between centers; make sure that the lathe and router are unplugged. Set the router's depth of cut so the bit is centered along the horizontal axis of the blank. Rotate the faceplate by hand until one of the flute lines is at the 12 o'clock position. Tighten a handscrew around the lathe drive shaft to prevent it from rotating.

To be certain that all the flutes will be the same length, clamp a stop block to the lathe bed. Butt

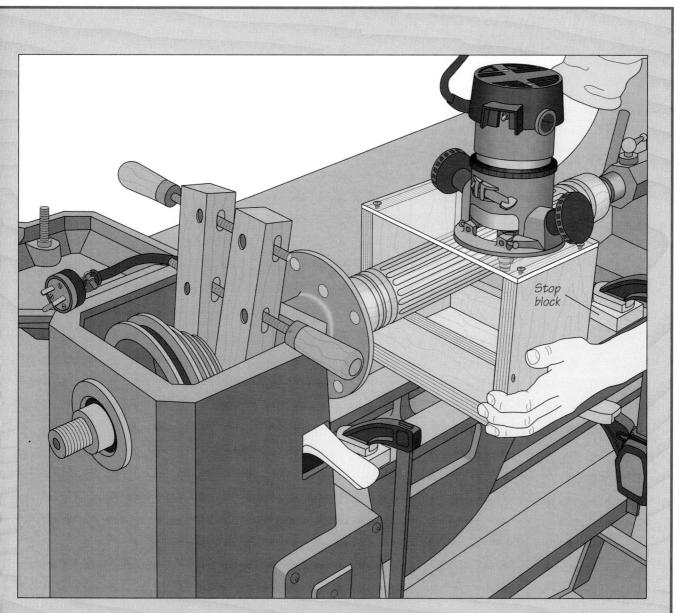

Stop block

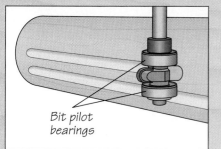

Bit pilot bearings

the jig against the headstock of the lathe, turn on the router, and push on the side of the jig to feed the bit into the blank. Once the pilots are bearing against the stock *(left)*, slide the jig along the lathe bed until it contacts the stop block. Keep the bit pilots pressed against the stock throughout the cut as it routs the flute.

Turn off the router, remove the handscrew, and rotate the faceplate by hand until the next flute line is at the 12 o'clock position. Reinstall the handscrew. Repeat to cut the remaining flutes *(above)*.

2 Setting up the tapering jig

To taper a leg with a router, use the jig shown at right, consisting of two tapering guides—one fixed and one adjustable—a plywood base, and two wedges. For the jig, cut a ¾-inch-wide, 1½-inch-deep rabbet along one edge of each guide, then screw one of the guides to the base so the rabbet is facing up. Holding the leg flush against the fixed guide, slip the wedges under the workpiece at each end so the taper start line on the face and the uppermost outline on the end are both level with the rabbet shoulder on the guide. Then butt the rabbeted face of the adjustable guide against the leg and clamp it in place so the ends of the guides are aligned.

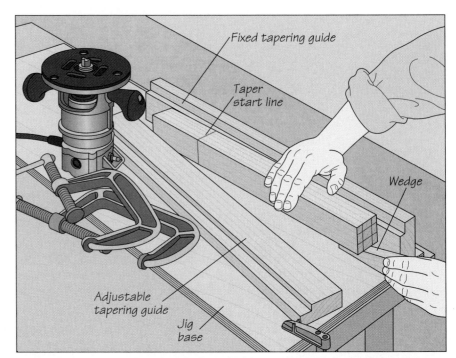

Fixed tapering guide

Taper start line

Wedge

Adjustable tapering guide

Jig base

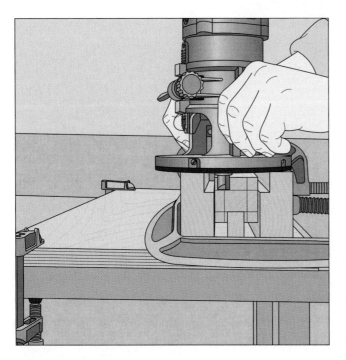

3 Tapering one side of the leg

Install a top-piloted ¾-inch straight bit in the router. To adjust the cutting depth, set the sub-base on the jig and extend the bit to the taper shoulder. Then turn on the tool and, starting at the top of the leg, remove the waste in straight passes toward the bottom *(above)*. Work from one edge of the leg to the other until the entire surface has been tapered.

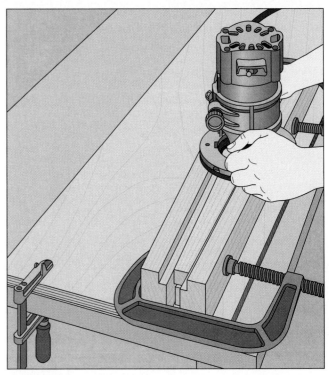

3 Finishing the taper

To taper the remaining three sides of the leg, unclamp the adjustable guide, rotate the workpiece in the jig by 90°, and reposition the wedge. Then resecure the guide and remove the waste as you did in step 3 *(above)*.

ROUTING REEDS ON A TURNED LEG

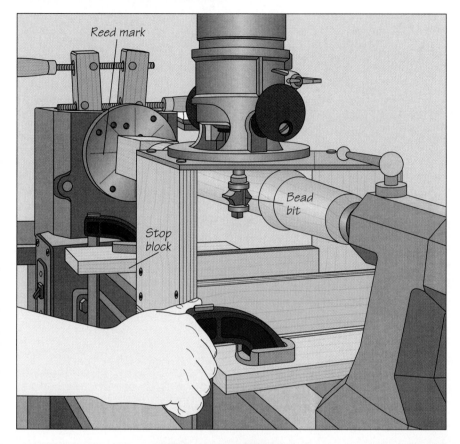

1 Routing the reeds

You can use your router along with the lathe-mounted jig shown on page 120 to cut reeds in a turned leg. For this operation, install a double-piloted bead bit in the router and, to ensure that the length of the reeds is uniform, clamp a stop block at each end of the lathe bed *(left)*. Make index marks for the reeds on the lathe faceplate, spacing the lines equally, and mount the leg on the lathe so the cut will start at the leg's thicker end as the router is fed against the direction of bit rotation. Once the setup is complete, rout the reeds as you would flutes *(page 121)*, guiding the jig and router against the direction of bit rotation from one stop block to the other to cut the reeds one after another *(below)*.

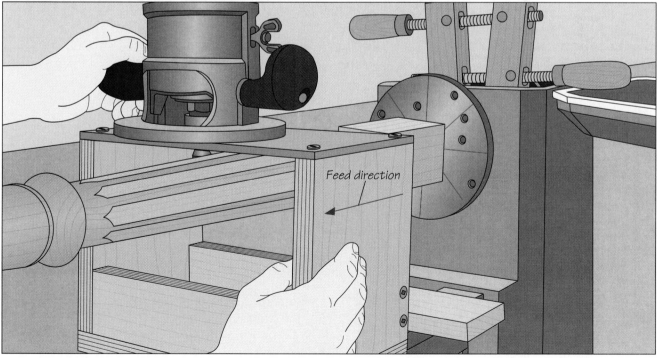

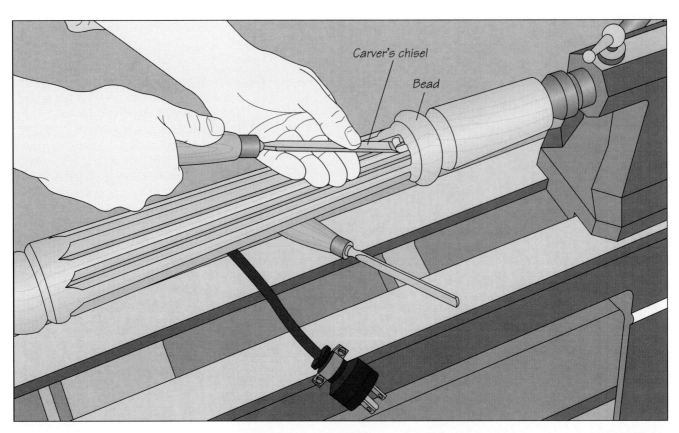

Carver's chisel

Bead

2 Finishing the reeds

The router cuts the waste between the reeds, leaving the top surfaces of the reeds flat and their ends straight. Finish carving the reeds by hand. To round over the top surface of the reeds, make a series of cuts on each side of the grooves between them, rolling a flat carver's chisel slightly from side to side. Follow the leg's contours, making the reeds wider at the top than at the bottom. At the bottom of the reeds, use the chisel to extend the grooves right to the next decorative element—in this case, a bead *(above)*—paring away the waste in thin layers. Round off the tops of the reeds by making a plunge cut with the appropriate-size carving gouge *(right)*.

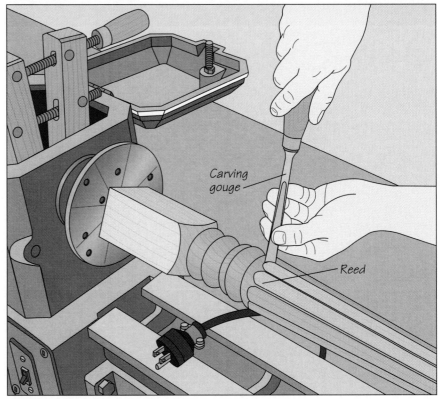

Carving gouge

Reed

SPIRALING A LEG

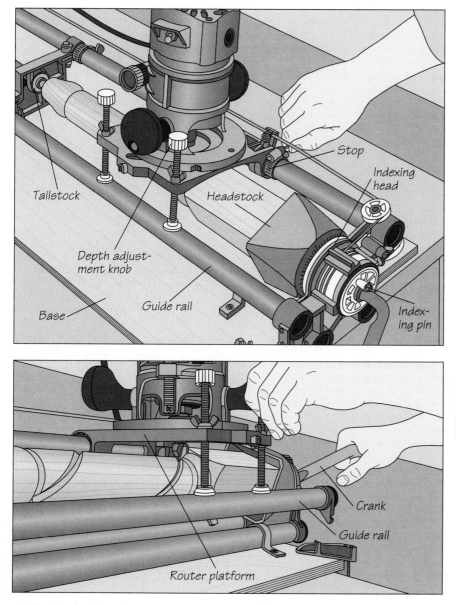

Tailstock

Headstock

Stop

Indexing head

Depth adjustment knob

Base

Guide rail

Indexing pin

Crank

Guide rail

Router platform

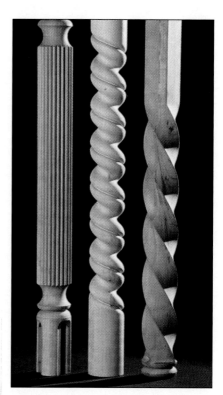

Each of the spiral designs on the legs shown above was cut by a router aided by a turning jig similar to the one illustrated at left. The jig holds a workpiece between centers, as on a lathe, and secures the router upright on a metal platform that can be adjusted for the desired depth of cut. The jig features a crank that rotates the workpiece, enabling the bit to cut all around the leg's circumference; the crank can also be used to simultaneously move the platform along the guide rails, producing a spiral cut.

Woodworkers traditionally cut spiral designs into legs by hand with carving gouges, after first drawing a grid on the workpiece and then marking the spiral with a pencil. The use of spiraling as a design element dates back to classical Roman architecture and, more recently, Georgian and Chippendale furniture made during the 18th Century.

1 Routing the first spiral
Fix the workpiece and router on the jig, adjusting the depth knobs so the router platform clears the stock. Set the router's cutting depth so the bit will penetrate the stock the desired amount when the knobs contact the guide rail. Next, use the jig indexing head and pin to evenly space the number of spirals. To ensure all the spirals will be the same length, rotate the crank to move the platform to the headstock end of the jig, butt the stop on the guide rail against the platform, and lock it in place *(above, top)*. Repeat with the stop at the other end. With the platform tilted up and butted against the stop at the tailstock end, turn on the router and lower the platform—plunging the bit into the stock—until the depth knobs contact the guide rail. Then turn the crank, rotating the workpiece and moving the platform, until the router reaches the headstock end *(above, bottom)*.

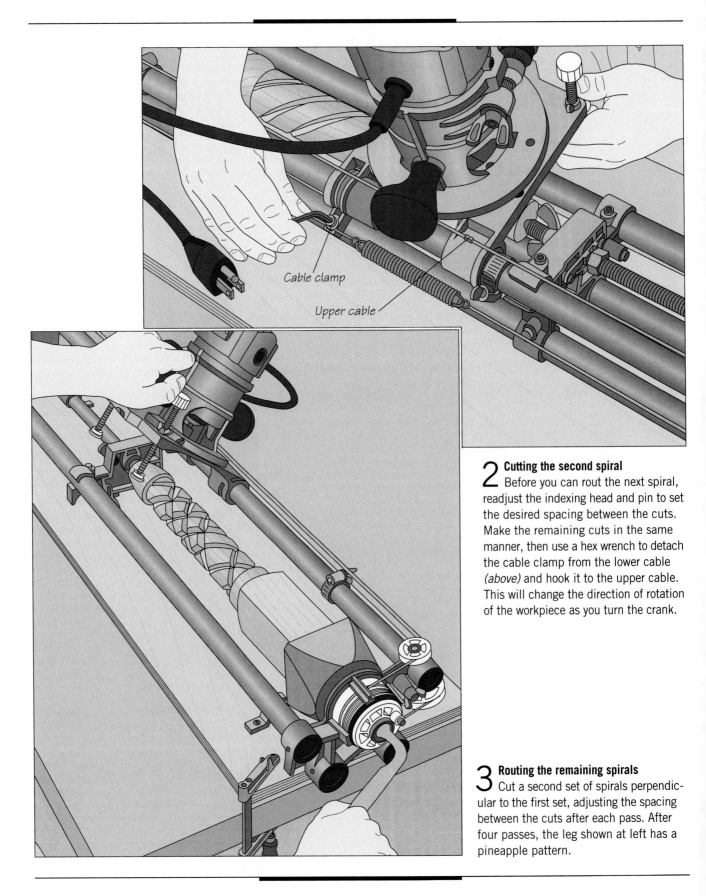

Cable clamp

Upper cable

2 Cutting the second spiral
Before you can rout the next spiral, readjust the indexing head and pin to set the desired spacing between the cuts. Make the remaining cuts in the same manner, then use a hex wrench to detach the cable clamp from the lower cable *(above)* and hook it to the upper cable. This will change the direction of rotation of the workpiece as you turn the crank.

3 Routing the remaining spirals
Cut a second set of spirals perpendicular to the first set, adjusting the spacing between the cuts after each pass. After four passes, the leg shown at left has a pineapple pattern.

CARVING WITH ROUTERS

Carving has traditionally been the exclusive domain of artisans wielding hand tools. But, armed with a router and one of the jigs shown in this section, you can produce carvings similar to hand-wrought works.

Although most plunge bits can be used in router-carving, some cutters have specific applications. With their capacity for removing large quantities of waste, bowl bits, for example, are ideal for relief carving. A V-bit can be used for producing serifs in lettering, while veining and lettering bits excel at creating the lines typical of incised letters. It is easiest to feed the router with a pulling motion, rather than pushing it along, so set up your operations accordingly.

There are few hard and fast rules in carving, so it is a good idea to practice your cuts on scrap material, particularly when you are routing freehand.

Secured in the bowl-carving jig shown at right, a router cuts decorative flutes on a goblet. The jig sits on the bed of a lathe, enabling the carving to be done without removing a turned piece from the machine. For details on making and using the jig, refer to page 130.

ROUTING A FAN CARVING

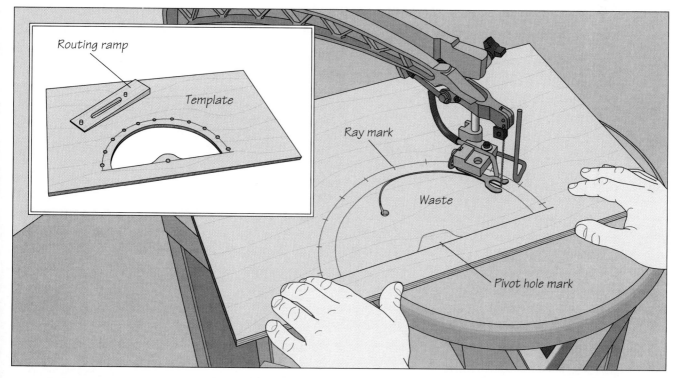

Routing ramp

Template

Ray mark

Waste

Pivot hole mark

1 Making the template
To carve a fan with a laminate trimmer, you need a two-piece jig consisting of a template and a routing ramp *(inset)*. For the template, use a compass to draw a semicircle of the desired diameter on a piece of ¼-inch plywood or hardboard. Draw a second semicircle from the same center about 1 inch larger than the first. Mark lines for the rays of the fan along the larger arc, spacing the marks equally. Also mark an area around the arc center; this will provide a solid bearing for the ramp point. Drill a hole for a scroll saw blade through the waste section of the template and set the stock on the saw table, then slip the blade through the hole and cut away the waste *(above)*. Drill a hole through the template at the pivot hole mark and each ray mark, using a bit of the same diameter as the dowels you will use in the ramp.

2 Making the routing ramp

Cut a 1-by-3 wood block a few inches longer than the fan rays you plan to carve. Rout a slot through it; the width of the slot should accommodate the template guide you will use on the laminate trimmer and the length should equal that of the fan rays. Starting a few inches from one end, bevel both faces of the block on your band saw so that it tapers to a thin wedge. Smooth the cut surfaces on a disk sander *(right)*. To finish preparing the ramp, mark a point on each side of the slot for dowels; the distance between the points should equal the gap between the pivot hole and the ray holes on the template. Drill the holes and glue a short length of dowel into each one. Trim the dowels flush with the ramp top.

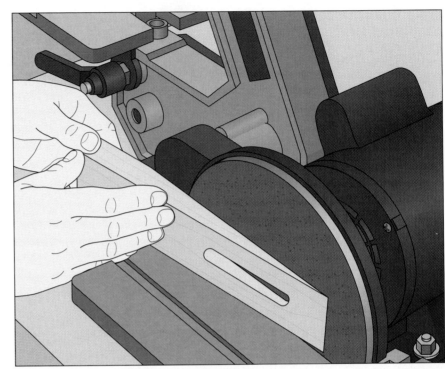

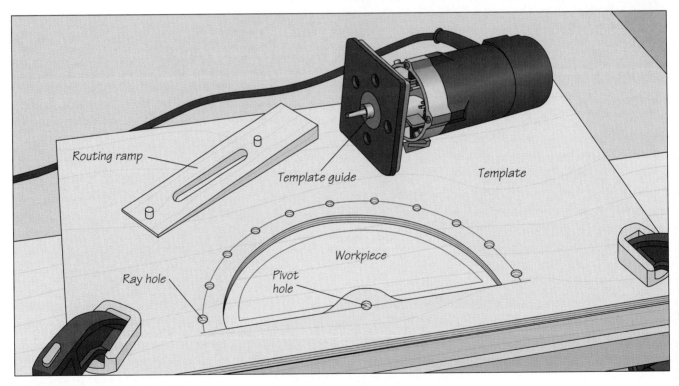

3 Setting up the jig and laminate trimmer

Install a straight bit or core box bit as well as a template guide in a laminate trimmer *(above)*. Then lay the workpiece on your benchtop and clamp the template on top. Set the routing ramp in position, fitting the dowel at its thick end in the pivot hole and the other dowel in the first ray hole.

4 Routing the first fan ray

Start by holding the laminate trimmer on the thick end of the ramp, tilting the base plate so the bit is clear of the stock. Then turn on the tool and pivot the cutter into the workpiece, butting the template guide at the end of the slot. Once the trimmer base plate is flat on the ramp, feed it down the ramp. Turn off the tool and tilt the base plate off the ramp once the template guide contacts the end of the slot *(left)*.

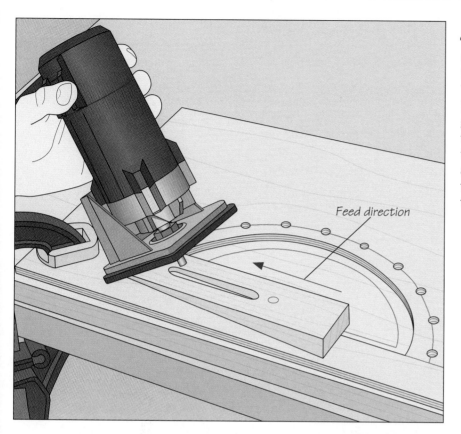

Feed direction

5 Cutting the remaining rays

Pivot the thin end of the ramp into the next ray hole. Then rout the ray the same way you cut the first one. Continue until all the rays are done *(below)*.

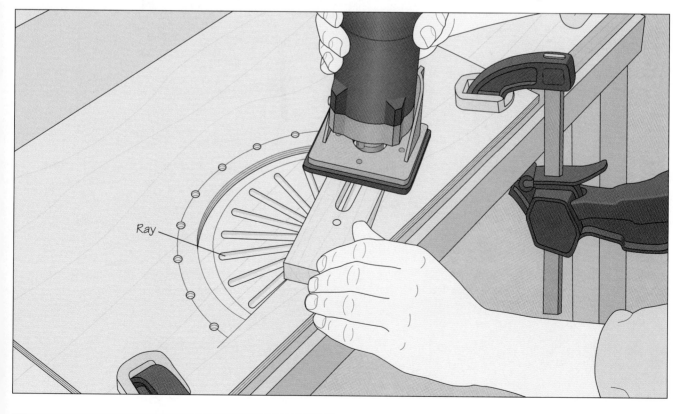

Ray

BOWL-CARVING JIG

Made entirely of ¾-inch plywood and a piece of ¼-inch clear acrylic, the jig shown at right will enable you to use your router to carve decorative features into faceplate turnings while they are still mounted on your lathe. The jig holds the router upright over the workpiece *(below)*, allowing the tool to pivot into the cut.

Prepare the jig so the base and sub-base are as long as the width of your lathe bed and wide enough to support the router. The sides of the jig should be high enough to hold the tool above the turning when the jig is set on the lathe bed. Starting halfway up the sides, drill a row of aligned holes for machine screws up the center of the boards at 1-inch intervals. Cut the braces and support arms as shown, drill holes through the arms near the

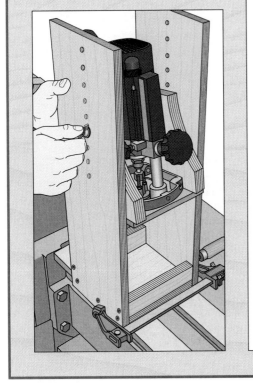

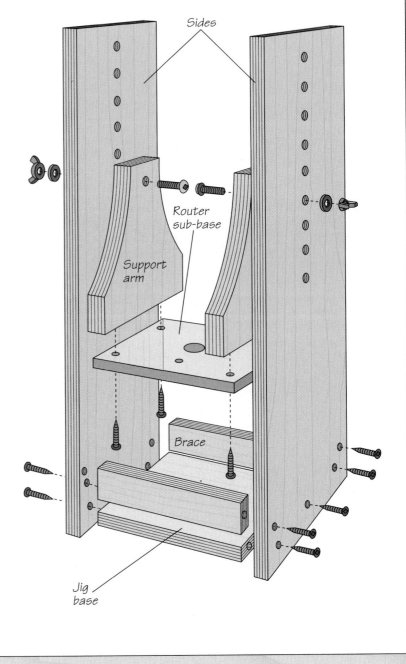

Sides

Router
sub-base

Support
arm

Brace

Jig
base

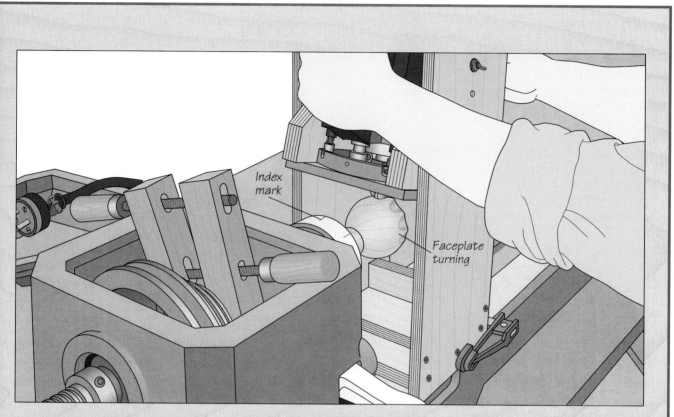

Index
mark

Faceplate
turning

top end, and assemble the jig, fasten-
ing the base and braces to the sides
and the sub-base to the support arms.
The bottom ends of the sides should
extend below the base and hug the
lathe bed.

To use the jig, set it on the lathe bed
so the turning is positioned between
the sides and clamp it securely. Attach
the router to the sub-base. Then
fasten the support arms to the sides
with machine screws, washers, and

wing nuts at a height that will enable
you to pivot the bit into the stock for
the desired cut; leave the wing nuts
loose enough for you to swivel the
arms. Adjust the bit's cutting depth.

To space the cuts equally, make
index marks on the lathe chuck.
Rotate the chuck by hand until one
of the marks is at the 12 o'clock position and tighten a handscrew around
the lathe drive shaft to prevent it from
rotating. To make the first cut, turn
on the router and pivot the arms of
the jig to plunge the bit into the stock
(above). Turn off the router, remove
the handscrew, and rotate the chuck
by hand to align the next index mark
with the bit, then reinstall the handscrew. Repeat until all the cuts are
done (left).

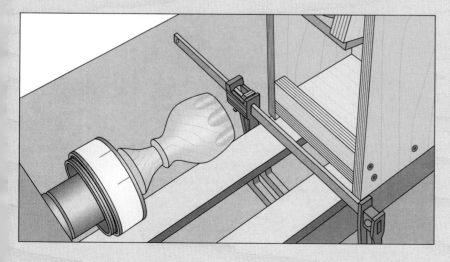

CARVING IN THE ROUND WITH THE ROUTER

1 Setting up the router and jig
Paired with a commercial pantograph like the one shown at right, a router fitted with a ⅛-inch veining bit can be used for carving in the round, or 3-D carving. Set up the router and jig following the manufacturer's instructions. The jig shown is screwed down to a work surface, while the workpiece and the pattern are secured with double-sided tape. The router is fastened to the jig's metal plate and the jig stylus is positioned above the pattern. As you guide the stylus across the surface of the pattern, the pantograph moves the router in the same direction by the same amount, enabling the bit to reproduce the pattern on the workpiece. With most jigs of this sort, you have to adjust the setup and the router's cutting depth *(below)* to ensure the bit will cut both the high and low points of the carving without gouging too deep or missing any areas.

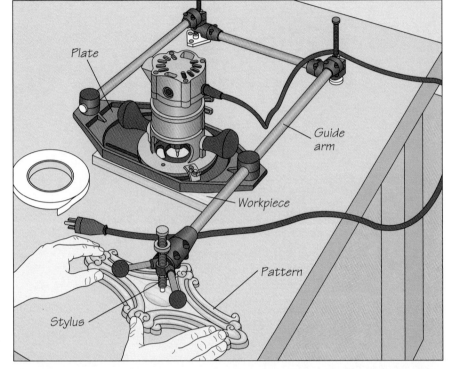

Plate

Guide arm

Workpiece

Pattern

Stylus

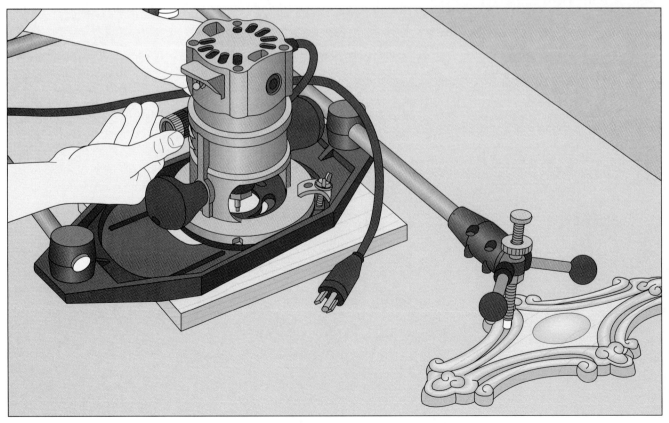

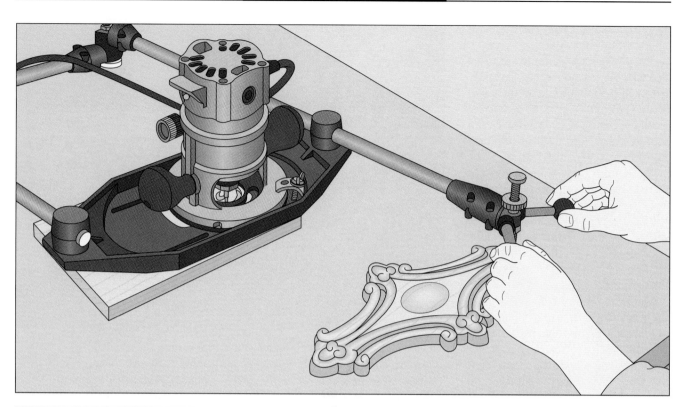

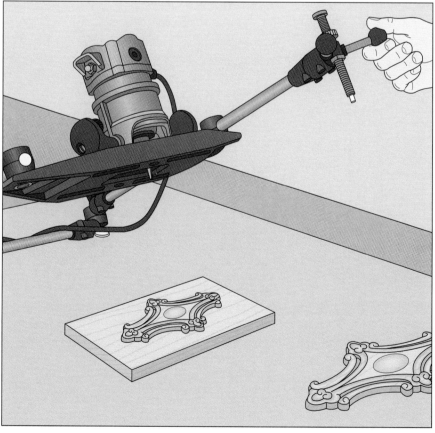

2 Duplicating the pattern

Turn on the router and grasp the handles adjoining the stylus firmly with both hands. Starting at one corner of the pattern, begin running the stylus slowly along the surface; the router bit will make a corresponding cut in the workpiece *(above)*. For best results, move from the high points of the pattern toward the low ones. To copy the pattern exactly, the stylus must cover all the pattern's surface; you can lift the jig and router off the workpiece periodically *(left)* to check your progress.

FREEHAND ROUTING

Freehand cutting with a router, guiding the tool only with steady eyes and hands, is similar to sculpture, requiring practice and patience. Although experience will help you settle on the wood species, methods, and types of bits that work best for you, even a novice can achieve satisfactory results—provided the routing is done with care.

Freehand routing will allow you to do relief cutting, which involves carving away the waste surrounding the pattern you want, leaving the raised form on the surface, as shown in the photo at right. You can also do incised cutting (page 138), in which the waste sections are the final product.

Until you become comfortable with the techniques of freehand routing, practice on scrap wood—and heed the suggestions and tips presented on page 135. The remaining pages of this section show how freehand routing can cut relief and incised lettering.

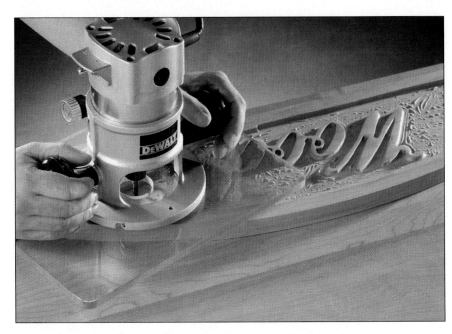

Fitted with a clear acrylic sub-base and a ¼-inch veining bit, a router is used freehand to carve lettering into a piece of wood. The sub-base is transparent so the user can view the cutting action, and it is wider than a standard sub-base to help keep the router steady on the workpiece.

FREEHAND ROUTER BITS

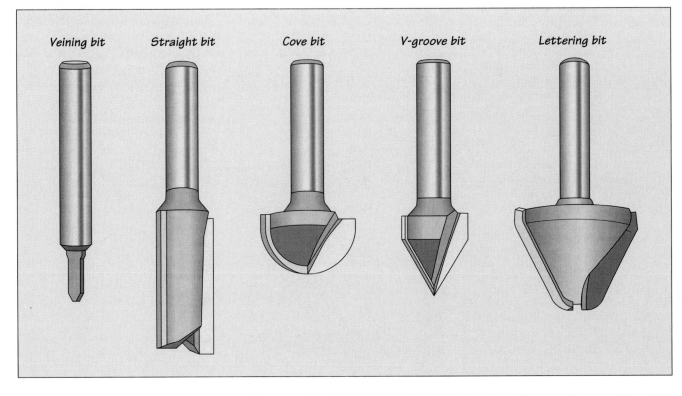

Veining bit   Straight bit   Cove bit   V-groove bit   Lettering bit

PRINCIPLES OF FREEHAND ROUTING

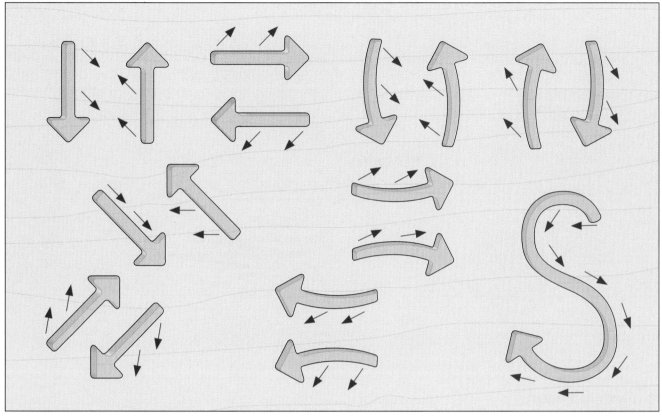

Illustration courtesy of Patrick Spielman

Guiding a router in freehand cutting

The large arrows in silhouette form in the illustration above represent several commonly used freehand router strokes, ranging from straight and diagonal cuts to gentle arcs and long, sinuous curves. The red arrows indicate the direction in which the router will tend to move as you make these cuts. To obtain the cut you want, you will have to counterbalance this tendency with feed pressure. With experience, applying the right amount of pressure in the proper direction will become second nature. For best results, always pull the router toward you, rather than pushing the tool into a cut. For deep cuts, it is best to make several intermediate passes. To minimize splintering, cut from waste sections toward uncut wood instead of the other way around. And avoid back strain by setting up your work at a comfortable height —which for most people is at the level of the base of the spine.

SAFETY TIPS

• Only use well-sharpened bits, and preferably ones that feature an anti-kickback design *(page 25).*

• Wear eye and ear protection.

• Avoid working when you are tired or under the influence of alcohol or medication.

• Make several shallow passes to complete a cut, rather than one deep cut.

• Apply adequate pressure to counter the router's pulling tendency.

• Install the bit in the router so that at least three-quarters of the shaft is in the collet.

• Hook up your router to a dust collection system.

• To avoid sudden distractions, keep pets, children, and onlookers away while you are working.

• Unplug your router whenever you are changing bits.

RELIEF CARVING WITH THE ROUTER

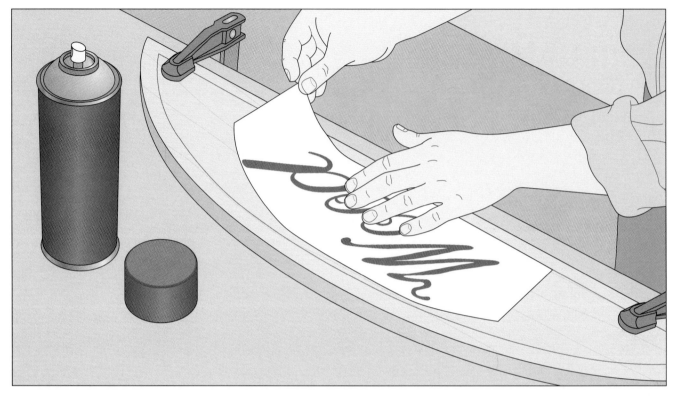

1 Transferring the pattern
Sketch or photocopy your pattern on a piece of paper and affix it to the workpiece *(above)*. If you use a spray adhesive, you will be able to peel the pattern off the surface when the carving is completed.

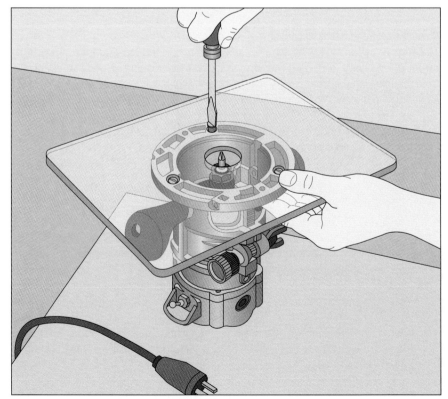

2 Making and installing an acrylic router sub-base
Replace the standard sub-base on your router with a clear acrylic one; this will enable you to view the cutting action as you rout the pattern. Cut the sub-base from ¼- or ⅜-inch-thick acrylic plastic, making the piece as large as necessary to keep the router steady on the workpiece; as a rule of thumb, the sub-base should be twice as wide as the workpiece. Use your standard sub-base as a template for drilling the bit clearance and screw holes through the acrylic, then fasten the sub-base to the router *(right)*.

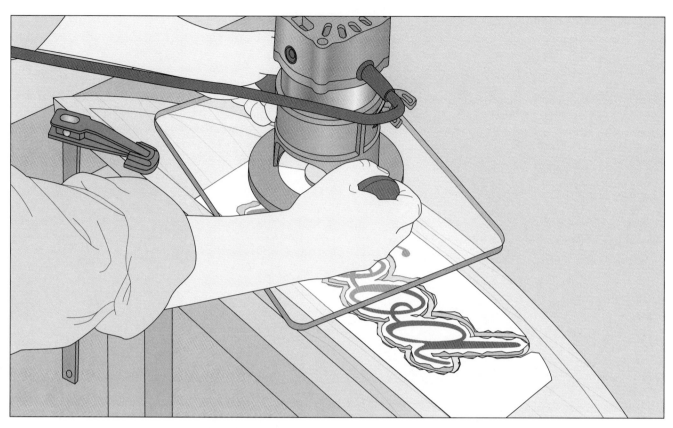

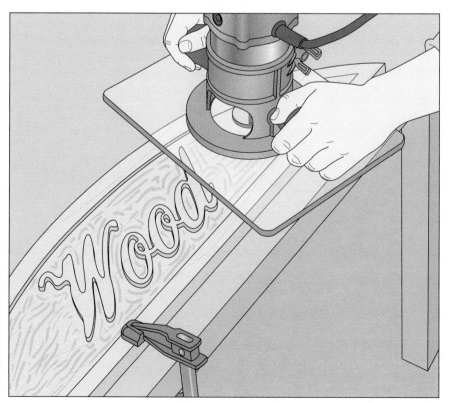

3 Defining the pattern

Install a small-diameter bit in your router; the cutter in the illustrations on this page is a ¼-inch veining bit. Starting at one end of the pattern, cut along its edges to remove the waste just outside the marked lines. Work on the outside edges of the pattern, then move on to the waste areas on the inside edges. Keep the sub-base flat on the workpiece throughout the operation *(above)*, guiding the router against the direction of bit rotation whenever possible.

4 Routing out the remaining waste

Feed the router in a series of back-and-forth, side-to-side passes to clear the waste remaining around the pattern. By varying the router's feed direction, you can impart a hand-carved texture to the workpiece *(left)*. Use a chisel, if necessary, to remove waste from tight spots.

ROUTING SERIF LETTERS

1 Outlining the letter patterns

Clamp your stock to a work surface and mark two parallel lines along the surface, spaced to equal the desired height of your letters. Then use a pencil to outline the letters on the surface. You can either sketch the letters freehand *(above)* or trace them from a pattern; for an elegant, traditional look, you can reproduce the old English letters shown below. Try to match the width of the letters' strokes to the diameter of the bit you will be using. To produce a traceable pattern of the appropriate size, use a photocopier with an enlargement feature; then, secure the finished pattern to the workpiece.

Guide line

AN ALPHABET OF OLD ENGLISH-STYLE SERIF LETTERS

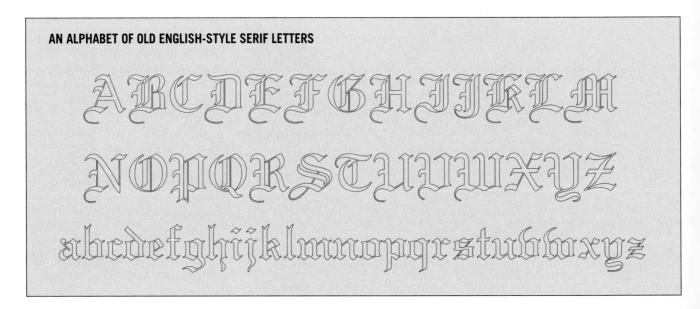

2 Making the straight cuts

Install a 60° V- bit in a laminate trimmer, set a shallow cutting depth, and start by routing the letters' straight elements; leave the serifs, or tail-like strokes on the top and bottom ends of the letters, for later *(step 3)*. Use a T-square jig to guide each cut; align the bit with the outline and butt the arm of the jig against the edge of the workpiece with the fence on the top surface and flush against the trimmer's base plate. Holding the jig in place, turn on the tool, plunge the bit into the stock at the beginning of the straight portion, and cut along it, pulling the trimmer toward you. Hold the base plate flat on the workpiece and flush against the edge guide throughout *(right)*.

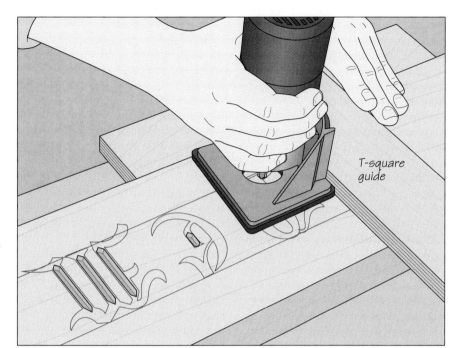

T-square guide

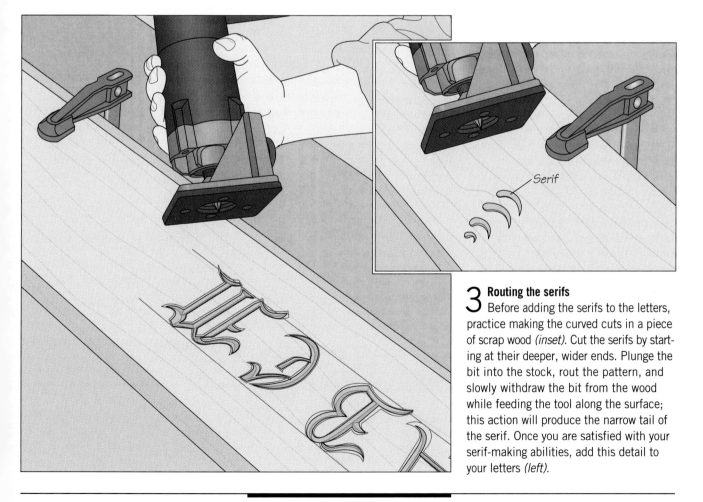

Serif

3 Routing the serifs

Before adding the serifs to the letters, practice making the curved cuts in a piece of scrap wood *(inset)*. Cut the serifs by starting at their deeper, wider ends. Plunge the bit into the stock, rout the pattern, and slowly withdraw the bit from the wood while feeding the tool along the surface; this action will produce the narrow tail of the serif. Once you are satisfied with your serif-making abilities, add this detail to your letters *(left)*.

GLOSSARY

A-B-C-D

Auxiliary fence: A wood fence attached to the standard fence of a router table; usually high enough to support a workpiece being fed across the table on end.

Blank: A length or block of wood used for turnings.

Bushing: In pattern routing, a small metal ring that snaps on and off a template guide to change its diameter.

Carbide-tipped bit: A router bit on which the cutting edges are made of a compound of tungsten and carbon; such cutting edges are stronger and stay sharper longer than conventional high-speed bits.

Caul: A board placed between clamps and the workpiece to distribute clamping pressure.

Cheek: In a mortise-and-tenon joint, the part of the tenon parallel to the board faces and perpendicular to the shoulder.

Chip-limiting bit: A bit that limits the depth of cut of the cutting edge; this reduces the risk of kickback, often caused by the larger gap of standard bits.

Collet: The sleeve on a router that holds the shank of a bit.

Cope-and-stick joint: A method of joining stiles and rails in frame-and-panel construction. The joint features mating tongues and grooves and a decorative molding along the inside edges of the boards.

Dado: A rectangular channel cut into a workpiece.

E-F-G-H-I-J

End grain: The arrangement and direction of the wood fibers viewed from the end of a board.

Featherboard: A piece of wood with thin fingers or "feathers" at one end; used in conjunction with clamps to hold a workpiece against the fence or top of a router table.

Fence: An adjustable guide on a router table to keep the edge, end, or face of a workpiece a set distance from the bit.

Flutes: Concave channels, usually evenly spaced, carved along the length of spindle turnings. See *reed*. Also, grooves in router bits that allow waste chips to be expelled.

Frame-and-panel assembly: A method of casework construction in which a wood panel floats in grooves in a frame made of horizontal rails and vertical stiles.

Indexing head: An accessory on some lathes that enables the headstock to be rotated manually in measured increments.

Infeed: The part of a router table that supports the workpiece before it reaches the bit.

Inlay: A decorative strip of metal, hardwood, or marquetry that is glued into a groove cut in a workpiece.

Jig: A device for guiding the router or holding a workpiece during an operation.

K-L-M-N-O-P-Q

Kerf: The space left when wood is removed by a cutter.

Kickback: The tendency of a workpiece to be thrown back in the direction of the operator of a tool.

Lathe capacity: The distance between centers on a lathe; limits the length of spindle work that can be mounted on the machine.

Medium-density fiberboard (MDF): A type of manufactured sheet material made from a wood fiber and resin composite; available in thicknesses from $1/4$ to 1 inch.

Miter gauge: As used in routing, this device slides in a slot to guide a workpiece over the bit; it can be set to various angles.

Molding: Decorative strips of wood that can be carved by the router.

Mortise-and-tenon joint: A joinery technique in which a projecting tenon cut in one board fits into a matching hole, or mortise, in another.

Mortise: A rectangular, circular or oval hole cut into a piece of wood.

Outfeed: The part of a router table that supports the work after it passes the bit during a cutting operation.

Pattern routing: A technique in which the workpiece is secured face-to-face to a template, and a piloted router bit or a template guide is fed along the template to reproduce its contours on the edge of the workpiece.

Pilot bearing: A free-spinning metal collar on a piloted router bit that follows the edge of a workpiece to maintain a uniform cutting depth or of a template to reproduce a shape.

Pilot hole: A hole drilled into a workpiece to prevent splitting when a screw is driven; usually made slightly smaller than the threaded section of the screw.

Pin router: A table assembly that suspends the router above the workpiece; a fence or pin on the table guides the workpiece under the bit.

Plunge router: A router whose motor assembly is mounted above the base of the tool on spring-loaded columns; downward pressure on the handles feeds or plunges the bit into the wood.

Push block or stick: A device used to feed a workpiece into a table-mounted router bit to protect the operator's fingers.

Pocket hole: An angled hole bored into the face of a workpiece and exiting from its end or edge; typically used to join frame rails and stiles, or table rails and tops.

Quarter column: A turned and sometimes fluted column set in niches in the front corners of highboys and other 18th-Century furniture.

R-S

Rabbet: A step-like cut in the edge or end of a board; usually forms part of a joint.

Rail: In a table, the boards that join the legs and support the top; in a chair, one of four boards that frame the seat. Also the horizontal member of a frame-and-panel assembly. See *stile.*

Raised panel: In frame-and-panel construction, a cabinet or door panel with beveled edges that creates the illusion that the central portion is "raised."

Reed: An evenly spaced, convex embellishment carved along the length of spindle turnings. See *flute.*

Runout: The amount of wobble that a router collet imparts to a bit when the tool is operating; 0.005 inch or less is acceptable.

Serif: The curved flourishes at the top and bottom ends of letters.

Shoulder: In a mortise-and-tenon joint, the part of the tenon perpendicular to the cheek. In a dovetail joint, the "valleys" between the pins and tails.

Sliding dovetail joint: A joinery method in which a dovetailed slide on one piece fits into a matching groove in the other.

Stile: The vertical member of a frame-and-panel assembly. See *rail.*

Stopped groove: A groove that stops before reaching the full length or width of a workpiece.

Tap: A hand tool used to cut spiral threads in wood or metal.

Tearout: The tendency of a cutter to tear the fibers of the wood it is cutting, leaving ragged edges, especially at the end or edge of the workpiece.

Template guide: A metal collar screwed onto a router's base plate to guide a non-piloted bit during a pattern routing operation.

Template: A pattern cut from plywood, hardboard, or particleboard allowing production of multiple identical copies of a part.

Tenon: A protrusion from the end of a workpiece that fits into a mortise.

Three-wing slotting cutter: A router bit designed to cut a narrow groove.

Through dovetail joint: A method of joining wood by means of interlocking pins and tails; the name derives from the distinctive shape cut into the ends of joining boards.

Tongue-and-groove joint: A joinery method featuring a protrusion from the edge or end of one board that fits into the groove of another.

Wood movement: The shrinking or swelling of wood in reaction to changes in relative humidity.

INDEX

Page references in *italics* indicate an illustration of subject matter. Page references in **bold** indicate a Build It Yourself project.

ACKNOWLEDGMENTS

The editors wish to thank the following:

ROUTERS AND ACCESSORIES
Adjustable Clamp Co., Chicago, IL; Birchall & Associates, Mississauga, Ont.; CMT Tools, Oldsmar, FL;
Delta International Machinery/Porter-Cable, Guelph, Ont.; DeWalt Industrial Tool Co.,
(Canada) Richmond Hill, Ont.; Linemaster Switch Corp., Woodstock, CT; Makita Canada Inc., Whitby, Ont.;
Milwaukee Electric Tool Corp., Brookfield, WI; Newman Tools, Inc., Montreal, Que.; Oak Park Enterprises, Ltd.,
Winnipeg, Man.; Robert Bosch Power Tools, Inc., (Canada) Mississauga, Ont.; Sears, Roebuck and Co., Chicago, IL;
Tool Trend Ltd., Concord, Ont.; Vermont American Corp., Lincolnton, NC and Louisville, KY; Patrick Warner,
Escondido, CA; Woodcraft Supply Corp., Parkersburg, WV; The Woodworker's Store, Rogers, MN

ROUTER BITS
Adjustable Clamp Co., Chicago, IL; American Tool Cos., Lincoln, NE;
CMT Tools, Oldsmar, FL; Delta International Machinery/Porter-Cable, Guelph, Ont.;
Diamond Machinery Technology, Inc., Marlborough, MA; Freud Westmore Tools, Ltd., Mississauga, Ont.;
Robert Bosch Power Tools, Inc., (Canada) Mississauga, Ont.

ROUTER TABLES
Adjustable Clamp Co., Chicago, IL; Black & Decker/Elu Power Tools, Towson, MD; CMT Tools, Oldsmar, FL;
Delta International Machinery/Porter-Cable, Guelph, Ont.; DeWalt Industrial Tool Co., (Canada)
Richmond Hill, Ont.; Freud Westmore Tools, Ltd., Mississauga, Ont.; Griset Industries, Inc., Santa Ana, CA;
NuCraft Tools, Clawson, MI; Porta-Nails, Inc., Wilmington, NC; Robert Bosch Power Tools, Inc.,
(Canada) Mississauga, Ont.; Sears, Roebuck and Co., Chicago, IL; Tool Trend Ltd., Concord, Ont.;
The Woodworker's Store, Rogers, MN

PATTERN ROUTING
Adjustable Clamp Co., Chicago, IL; CMT Tools, Oldsmar, FL; Delta International Machinery/Porter-Cable,
Guelph, Ont.; Design Forms Etc. Inc., Waterford, MI; David Keller, Petaluma, CA;
Makita Canada Inc., Whitby, Ont.; Ken Picou Design, Austin, TX; Shopsmith, Inc., Dayton, OH,
and Montreal, Que.; Spielman's Wood Works, Fish Creek, WI; Tool Trend Ltd., Concord, Ont.;
Wainbee Ltd., Pointe Claire, Que./DE-STA-CO, Troy, MI; Pat Warner, Escondido, CA

JOINERY
Adjustable Clamp Co., Chicago, IL; CMT Tools, Oldsmar, FL; Delta International Machinery/Porter-Cable,
Guelph, Ont.; DeWalt Industrial Tool Co., (Canada) Richmond Hill, Ont.;
Martin Godfrey, Wells, Somerset, UK; Great Neck Saw Mfrs. Inc. (Buck Bros. Division), Millbury, MA;
David Keller, Petaluma, CA; Leigh Industries Inc., Port Coquitlam, B.C.;
Taylor Design Group, Dallas, TX; Sears, Roebuck and Co., Chicago, IL;
Spielman's Wood Works, Fish Creek, WI; Tool Trend Ltd., Concord, Ont.

DECORATIVE TECHNIQUES
Adjustable Clamp Co., Chicago, IL; American Tool Cos., Lincoln, NE; Beall Tool Co., Newark, OH;
Delta International Machinery/Porter-Cable, Guelph, Ont.; DeWalt Industrial Tool Co., (Canada)
Richmond Hill, Ont.; Great Neck Saw Mfrs. Inc. (Buck Bros. Division), Millbury, MA; Phantom Engineering,
Provo, UT; S/J Fine Woodworks, Otis Orchards, WA; Sears, Roebuck and Co., Chicago, IL; Spielman's Wood
Works, Fish Creek, WI; Tool Trend Ltd., Concord, Ont.; Woodworker's Supply, Inc., Casper, WY

The following persons also assisted in the preparation of this book:
Lorraine Doré, Alan Flegg, Philip Lowe, Geneviève Monette

PICTURE CREDITS

Cover Robert Chartier
6, 7 Marie Louise Deruaz
8, 9 Tony Hutchings
10, 11 Ed Homonylo/Mammoth
37 Courtesy NuCraft Tools
111, 125 Courtesy Phantom Engineering